Literacy Plus

B

Language • Lifeskills • Civics

Joan Saslow

Consultants

Lisa Agao *California*	Robert Breitbard *Florida*	Virginia A. Cabasa-Hess *Illinois*	Janet S. Fischer *Massachusetts*	Carol Garcia *Illinois*
Glenda Gartman *California*	David L. Red *Virginia*	Lynn Reed *Arizona*	Margaret B. Silver *Missouri*	Gordon Thomas *Virginia*

Edwina Hoffman

Series Advisor

Longman

Literacy Plus B: Language, Lifeskills, Civics

Pearson Education, 10 Bank Street, White Plains, NY 10606

Vice president of instructional design: Allen Ascher
Senior acquisitions editor: Marian Wassner
Development editor: Martin Yu
Vice president, director of design and production: Rhea Banker
Executive managing editor: Linda Moser
Senior production editor: Christine Lauricella
Production manager: Liza Pleva
Director of manufacturing: Patrice Fraccio
Senior manufacturing buyer: Dave Dickey
Cover design: Ann France
Cover credit: Dollar Bills from "Cash, Coins & Currency" Disc © Comstock Images
Text design and composition: Wendy Wolf, Kim Teixeira, and Inez Sovjani
Illustrations: John Amoss, pp. 27, 28, 31, 32, 45, 46, 57, 63, 69, 70, 76, 77, 87, 88, 101, 106, 107, 110, 117, 119, 120, 123, 124, 127, 134, 138, 139, 150, 161, 173, 174, 175, 177, 178, 181, 182; Burmar Technical Corporation, pp. 2, 3, 19, 23, 26, 32, 50, 58, 85, 90, 91, 132, 148, 161, 178; Len Ebert, pp. 2, 18, 26, 36, 43, 46, 50, 58, 72, 73, 75, 97, 104, 121, 129, 135, 144, 151, 157, 166, 171, 176, 183; Seitu Hayden, pp. 10, 22, 28, 39, 53, 61, 64, 82, 89, 99, 108, 115, 122, 130, 131, 136, 137, 147, 148, 153, 158, 169, 175, 176, 184; Don Martinetti, pp. 13, 14, 17, 31, 40, 54, 76, 81, 85, 90, 94, 100, 125, 132, 140, 141, 154, 162, 179; Steve Sullivan, pp. 49, 53, 58, 67, 78, 81, 83, 84, 91, 95, 96, 102, 103, 104, 105, 109, 110, 117, 123, 128, 142, 147; Jill Wood, pp. 1, 8, 9, 21, 25, 32, 48, 49, 57, 68, 71, 79, 79, 86, 93, 103, 111, 112, 118, 125, 126, 133, 143, 155, 165, 172, 180, 187; Word & Image Design, pp. 35, 39, 86, 89, 100, 129, 132, 143, 149, 158, 163, 164, 165, 167, 170, 180, 186, 188

Library of Congress Cataloging-in-Publication Data

Saslow, Joan M.
  Literacy plus: language, lifeskills, civics. Level B/ Joan Saslow.
  p. cm.
ISBN 0-13-048416-4
1. English language--Textbooks for foreign speakers. 2. Life skills--Problems, exercises, etc. 3. Work--Problems, exercises, etc. I. Title.

PE1128 .S275 2003
428.2'4--dc21   2002031278

5 6 7 8 9 10—RRD—08 07

Printed in the United States of America

Table of contents

What is *Literacy Plus*?

Literacy Plus: Language, Lifeskills, Civics is a two-level adult course in English as a second language which starts at absolute beginner language and literacy level.

Learner profile

Written for adult immigrant learners, *Literacy Plus B* is for students who are becoming literate in English and who don't speak English. Recognizing the reality that adults can't wait to become literate in order to work and carry on their lives, *Literacy Plus* offers instruction in survival English, basic literacy, and elemental civics concepts at the same time.

Unit structure

Within each of the 10 units, alternating pages are entitled "Survival" or "Literacy." In this way, students make daily progress on their pathway to literacy, communication, and mastery of the civics concepts that enable them to interact confidently with others in the American community and workplace. A tinted "Teacher" box at the bottom of each page clearly describes the goal and content of the page.

Learner placement and progress

Students may be placed in *Literacy Plus A* or *Literacy Plus B*, according to their level of literacy. Students who are preliterate in their native language should be placed in *Literacy Plus A*. Students who have completed *Literacy Plus A* should then continue in *Literacy Plus B*. Students who are literate in their own language but not in English can begin in *Literacy Plus B*. A Placement Test can clarify a student's literacy level and appropriate placement.

Components of the *Literacy Plus* course

- **Student's Book.** A 10-unit student text contains daily lessons and practice in a convenient text-workbook format. A reference section at the back contains a complete phonics index, a complete guide to the survival language in the text, and an alphabetical list of vocabulary.
- **Audiocassettes.** A complete audio program contains listening and speaking practice of all vocabulary and conversations, as well as essential and effective listening comprehension exercises that prepare students to respond to authentic language outside of class.
- **Teacher's Edition.** A user-friendly wraparound edition contains daily lesson plans, teaching instructions, and complete tapescripts. Included in the Teacher's Edition is a CD-ROM with **Extra Practice Worksheets, Performance-based Achievement Tests,** and a **Placement Test**. These may be printed and duplicated as needed.
- **Flashcards.** These photocopiable cards allow group presentation, pair and group work games, as well as reinforcement of vocabulary, conversation, and literacy skills. They are packaged with the Teacher's Edition.
- **Guide for Native-Language Tutors.** A short guide enables a native-language tutor or classroom aide to enrich the civics strand by featuring it in the student's native language.

Scope and sequence

Unit	Literacy	Survival Language	Civics Concepts	Vocabulary
1 page 9	• Understand, identify, say, and write numbers 1–100. • Understand sequence of numbers. • Understand the numerical sequence of pages in a book.	• Make introductions. • State first, middle, and last name. • Use titles Mr. and Ms. • Exchange information about occupation. • Verify and confirm information. • Express and acknowledge thanks. • Give and respond to a compliment.	• Shake hands, exchange names, and express friendliness upon meeting someone new. • It's OK to compliment another person, even someone you don't know well. • Jobs are not determined by gender. • It's polite to ask about another's health. • It's important to say thanks when someone asks about your health.	• Occupations.
2 page 27	• Recognize, read, and say all the capital letters of the alphabet. • Trace and write all the capital letters of the alphabet, using left-to-right and top-to-bottom directionality.	• Give and get directions to a place. • Understand and state address, including zip code. • Clarify questions. • Ask for repetition.	• It's OK to ask a stranger for directions. • It's polite to provide friendly help to strangers asking for directions.	• Places in the community. • Types of housing.
3 page 45	• Recognize, trace, and write all the lowercase letters of the alphabet. • Fill out forms with both names, written in capital and lowercase letters, as well as area code and telephone number. • Understand touch pad and rotary telephone dials.	• Get information about public transportation. • Ask for and give driving directions to a place. • Ask for and give a telephone number. • Ask for clarification.	• Public transportation is named and numbered. • It's OK to ask police for directions. • Each telephone number has an area code for the region. You need an area code for calls outside of your own area code.	• Means of transportation.
4 page 63	• Recognize cursive capital and lowercase letters. • Sign one's own name in cursive capital and lowercase letters. • Recognize sound-symbol correspondence and trace initial consonants of known words.	• Ask for and express location of items in a store. • Talk about clothes and sizes. • Ask for and offer help. • Apologize. • Verify identity.	• Salespeople expect you to ask them about the location of items in a store. • Clothing sizes are either relative [small, medium, etc.] or by standard numbers. • Salespeople expect to get items in sizes that customers can't get for themselves. • Customers are entitled to service in a retail store, but from the appropriate person.	• Clothing. • Sizes. • Types of stores.
5 page 81	• Recognize sound-symbol correspondence of the short vowel sounds in minimal pairs. • Recognize short vowel sounds when following initial consonant blends. • Write one's own date of birth on a form, using numerals for the month, day, and year. • Understand and connect abbreviations with words for days of the week and months of the year.	• Ask for and give times. • Talk about daily schedules. • Discuss work schedules. • Ask for and give country of origin. • Make suggestions. • Talk about the weather. • Exchange greetings for times of day.	• It's OK to ask strangers for the time. • Work and school times are regular, scheduled events. Be aware of them. • Show interest in the activities of others and offer information about oneself. • Weather is a common topic in making friendly small talk.	• Times of day and clock times. • Days of the week. • Months of the year. • Daily activities. • Weather expressions.

Unit	Literacy	Survival Language	Civics Concepts	Vocabulary
6 page 99	• Recognize and decode rhyming and non-rhyming one-syllable words with short vowels, final consonants, and initial consonants and consonant blends. • Produce corresponding sounds in new words.	• Talk about food and meals. • Make a shopping list. • Discuss healthfulness of foods. • Discuss schedules. • Suggest a course of action. • Express likes. • Agree.	• Respect schedules. • Don't reach for things at the table; rather, ask others politely to pass them. • Be aware of healthfulness of foods and guide children to make good food decisions.	• Meals. • Common foods, drinks, and condiments.
7 page 117	• Decode one-syllable words with short vowels and initial and final consonant blends and digraphs. • Decode one-syllable plurals, both voiceless and voiced. • Read, understand, and fill out a form requesting personal information, including gender.	• Provide a social security number and marital status. • Answer a telephone at work. • Take and leave telephone messages. • Express a belief. • Express lack of understanding.	• Expect to provide social security numbers and marital status in public offices. • Take responsibility for members of family. • Inform your employer when you're going to be late.	• Rooms in the house. • Family relationships. • Marital status.
8 page 135	• Identify and understand common warning, safety, and traffic signs. • Leave a space between words. • Leave a space between first and last names. • Use capital and lowercase letters for names. • Write on the line, not above or below the line.	• Describe an injury. • Inquire about a misfortune. • Tell about one's illness. • State an emergency. • Call 911. • Express and accept sympathy. • Ask for and provide a reason.	• Inform employer when you can't come to work and provide a legitimate reason. • Follow a sequence of directions before getting medical or dental attention. • There are laws requiring seat belt use and safety restraints. Observe the law.	• Parts of the body. • Common ailments and injuries. • Emergency vehicles and medical personnel. • Health care facilities.
9 page 153	• Understand monetary equivalents of U.S. currency and write dollar and cent amounts. • Write a name and address on an envelope, using capital and lowercase letters, conventional three-line format, and spaces between words.	• Ask for change. • Agree and decline to rent. • Ask about what's included in the rent. • Make payment with cash, check, money order, and credit card. • Show I.D. upon request. • Request a receipt.	• It's OK to ask a stranger for change. • Rental agreements vary with what's included in the rent. Inquire before signing. • You are expected to provide I.D. to write a personal check. • It's important to get a receipt for purchases.	• Coin and bill names. • Household bills. • Forms of payment.
10 page 171	• Decode words with r-controlled vowels, long vowels followed by consonants and mute e, and diphthongs. • Begin sentences with a capital letter and end with a period. • Leave a space between sentences. • Fill out a job application with personal information.	• Describe place of employment or state of temporary unemployment. • Describe one's job skills. • Provide information about past jobs and experience. • Complete a job application. • Express desire. • Express job preferences. • Offer references.	• Reading, writing, and speaking English (as well as other languages) are essential skills for success. • Matching your skills to those required on a job is important to finding employment. • Get references from employers in order to find future employment. • It's OK to ask for explanations or repetition of instructions that you don't understand.	• Occupations. • Workplaces. • Employment skills.

Joan Saslow

Joan Saslow has taught English as a second language and English as a foreign language to adults and young adults in the United States and Chile. She taught workplace English at the General Motors auto assembly plant in Tarrytown, NY; and Adult ESL at Westchester Community College and at Marymount College in New York. In addition, Ms. Saslow taught English and French at the Binational Centers of Valparaíso and Viña del Mar, Chile, and the Catholic University of Valparaíso.

Ms. Saslow is the author of the *Workplace Plus* and *Ready to Go* series for adult ESL students. She is the series director of Longman's popular five-level adult course *True Colors, an EFL Course for Real Communication* and of *True Voices*, a five-level video course. She is also author of *English in Context: Reading Comprehension for Science and Technology*, a three-level series for English for special purposes. In addition, Ms. Saslow has been an editor of language teaching materials, a teacher trainer, and a frequent speaker at gatherings of ESL and EFL teachers for over thirty years.

Series advisor
Edwina Hoffman

Edwina Hoffman has taught English for speakers of other languages in South Florida and at the Miccosukee Tribe of Indians, and English as a foreign language in Venezuela. She provided teacher training in a seven-state area for federally funded multi-functional resource centers serving the southeastern part of the United States. Dr. Hoffman taught English composition at Florida International University and graduate ESOL methods at the University of Miami.

Dr. Hoffman is an instructional supervisor with the adult and vocational programs of Miami-Dade County Public Schools in Miami, Florida. She has acted as a consultant, reviewer, and author of adult ESOL materials for over twenty years. A graduate of Middlebury College, Dr. Hoffman's doctoral degree is from Florida International University.

Welcome

🎧 **Look and listen.**

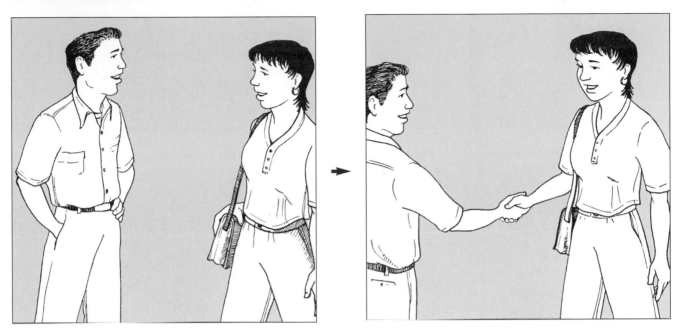

🎧 **Listen again and repeat.**

Pair work.

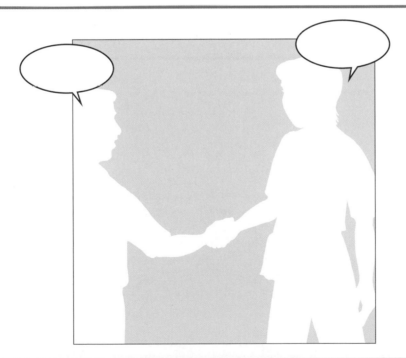

Look.

 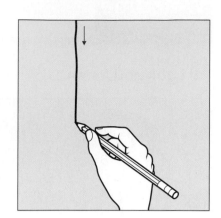 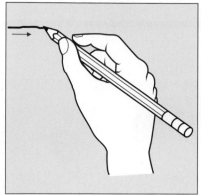

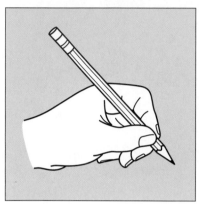 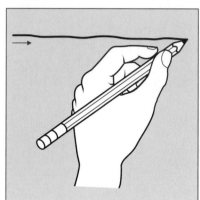 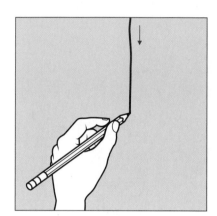

Trace.

TEACHER

Literacy: Hold pencil and pen in preferred hand. See left-to-right and top-to-bottom directionality.

2 • WELCOME

Look.

Trace.

* Teacher: Write student's name in bottom portion of name tag.

Literacy: A name is written with symbols. Trace one's own name.
More practice: Worksheet 1 (Teacher's Edition CD-ROM).

TEACHER

Trace.

TEACHER

Literacy: Practice tracing lines from left to right and top to bottom, in a variety of lengths.
More practice: Worksheet 2 (Teacher's Edition CD-ROM).

4 • WELCOME

Circle.

Cross out.

Match.

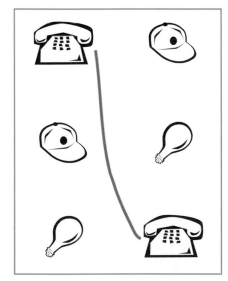 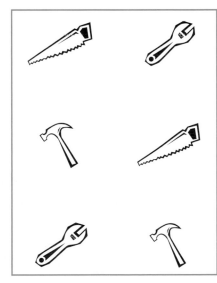 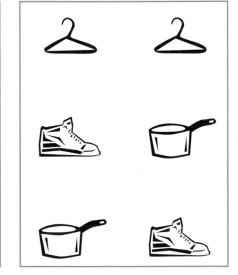

TEACHER

Literacy: Copy circling, crossing out, and matching from left to right and top to bottom.
More practice: Worksheet 3 (Teacher's Edition CD-ROM).

Circle.

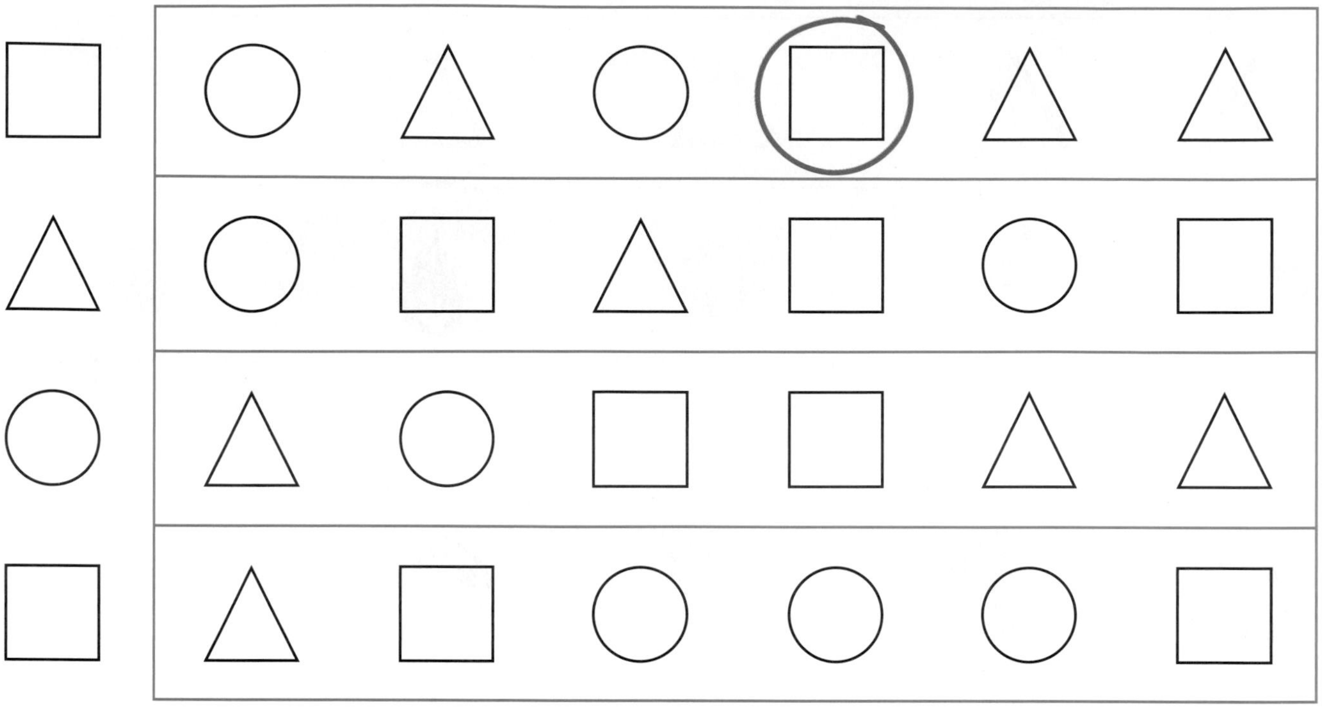

Cross out.

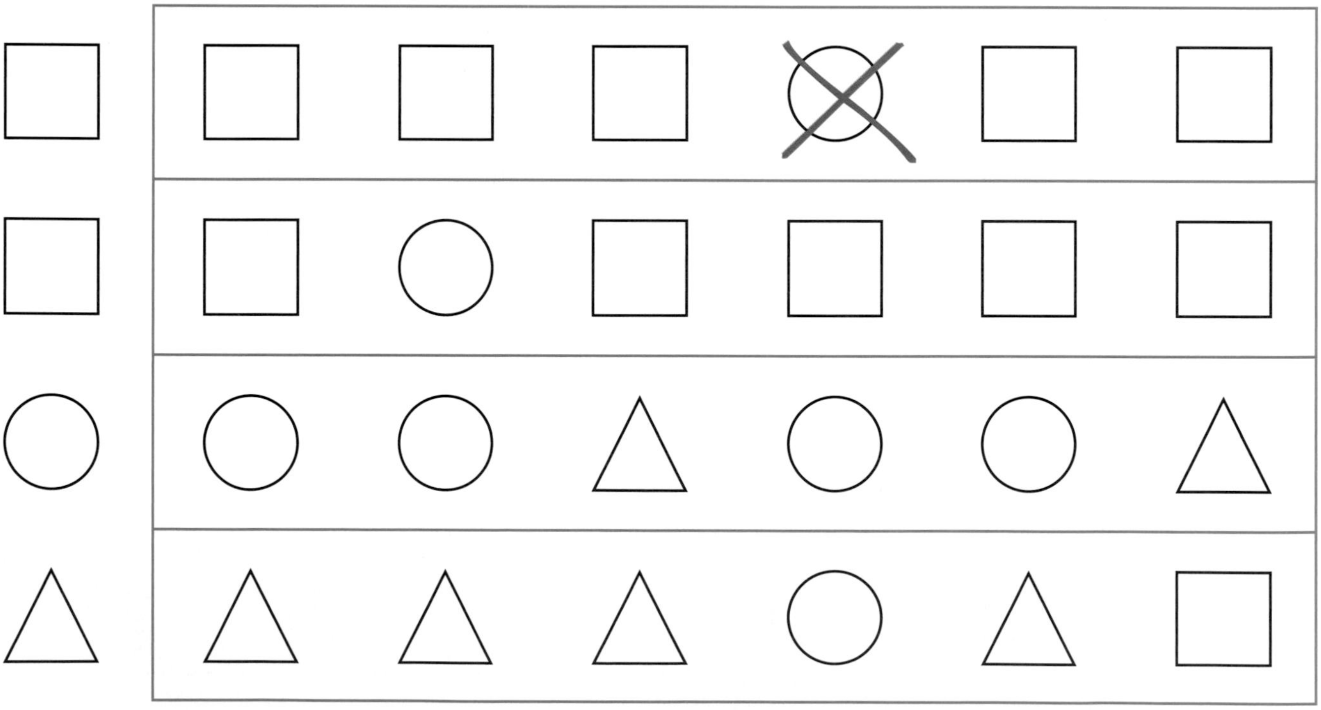

TEACHER

Literacy: Recognize square, triangle, and circle. Demonstrate ability to circle shape that is same and cross out shape that is different in a group.
More practice: Worksheet 4 (Teacher's Edition CD-ROM).

Trace.

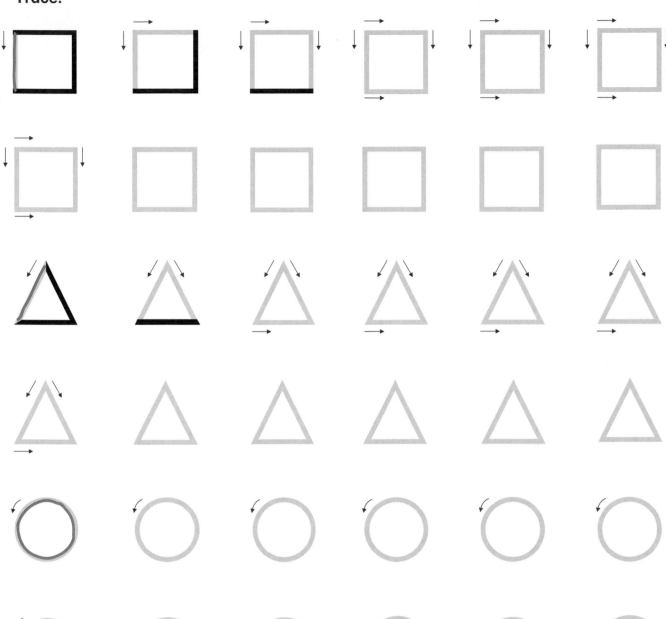

Literacy: Trace square, triangle, and circle, using left-to-right and top-to-bottom directionality.
More practice: Worksheet 5 (Teacher's Edition CD-ROM).

TEACHER

NAME

🎧 Look and listen.

🎧 Listen again and repeat.

Pair work.

🎧 **Look and listen.**

🎧 **Listen again and repeat.**

Pair work.

TEACHER

Survival: Make informal introductions.
Civics concepts: Shake hands, exchange names, and express friendliness upon meeting someone new. Use first names in informal settings.
New language: Hi. I'm [Ted]. / Nice to meet you [too].

🎧 **Look and listen.**

NANCY LEE
NAME

🎧 **Listen again and repeat.**

Pair work.

TEACHER

Survival: Ask about names. Express and acknowledge thanks.
Civics concept: Give both first and last name in formal settings.
New language: What's your name? / Thank you. / You're welcome.

🎧 **Look and listen.**

1	■
2	■ ■
3	■ ■ ■
4	■ ■ ■ ■
5	■ ■ ■ ■ ■
6	■ ■ ■ ■ ■ ■
7	■ ■ ■ ■ ■ ■ ■
8	■ ■ ■ ■ ■ ■ ■ ■
9	■ ■ ■ ■ ■ ■ ■ ■ ■
10	■ ■ ■ ■ ■ ■ ■ ■ ■ ■

🎧 **Listen again and repeat.**

Look.

1 → 2 → 3 → 4 → 5 → 6 → 7 → 8 → 9 → 10

TEACHER

Literacy: Understand that a number represents a quantity. Learn and say the names of the numbers. Recognize symbols for quantities of 1–10. Recognize that numbers represent sequence.

Circle the number.

📖 (book)	(1)	3
📬📬 (mailboxes)	1	2
📎📎📎📎 (paper clips)	2	4
📚📚📚📚📚📚 (books)	6	10
☎☎☎☎ (phones)	4	3
📁📁📁📁📁 (folders)	7	5
🖊🖊🖊🖊🖊🖊🖊🖊 (pens)	6	9
📎📎📎📎📎📎📎📎📎📎 (paper clips)	10	7
✏✏✏✏✏✏✏✏ (pencils)	4	8
📚📚📚📚 (books)	4	3
☎ (phone)	1	7

Literacy: Recognize and understand symbols representing 1–10.
More practice: Worksheet 6 (Teacher's Edition CD-ROM).

🎧 Look and listen.

🎧 Listen again and repeat.

Pair work.

TEACHER

Survival: State last names. Give and respond to an informal compliment.
Civics concepts: It's OK to compliment another person, even someone you don't know well. Say thanks when you are complimented.
New language: That's a nice name. / Thanks!

🎧 **Look and listen.**

🎧 **Listen again and repeat.**

🎧 **Look and listen.**

Mr.   Ms.

🎧 **Listen again and repeat.**

Pair work.

Trace and write.

1 | 1 1 1 1 1 1 1

1 | 1

2 | 2 2 2 2 2 2 2

2 | 2

3 | 3 3 3 3 3 3 3

3 | 3

4 | 4 4 4 4 4 4 4

4 | 4

5 | 5 5 5 5 5 5 5

5 | 5

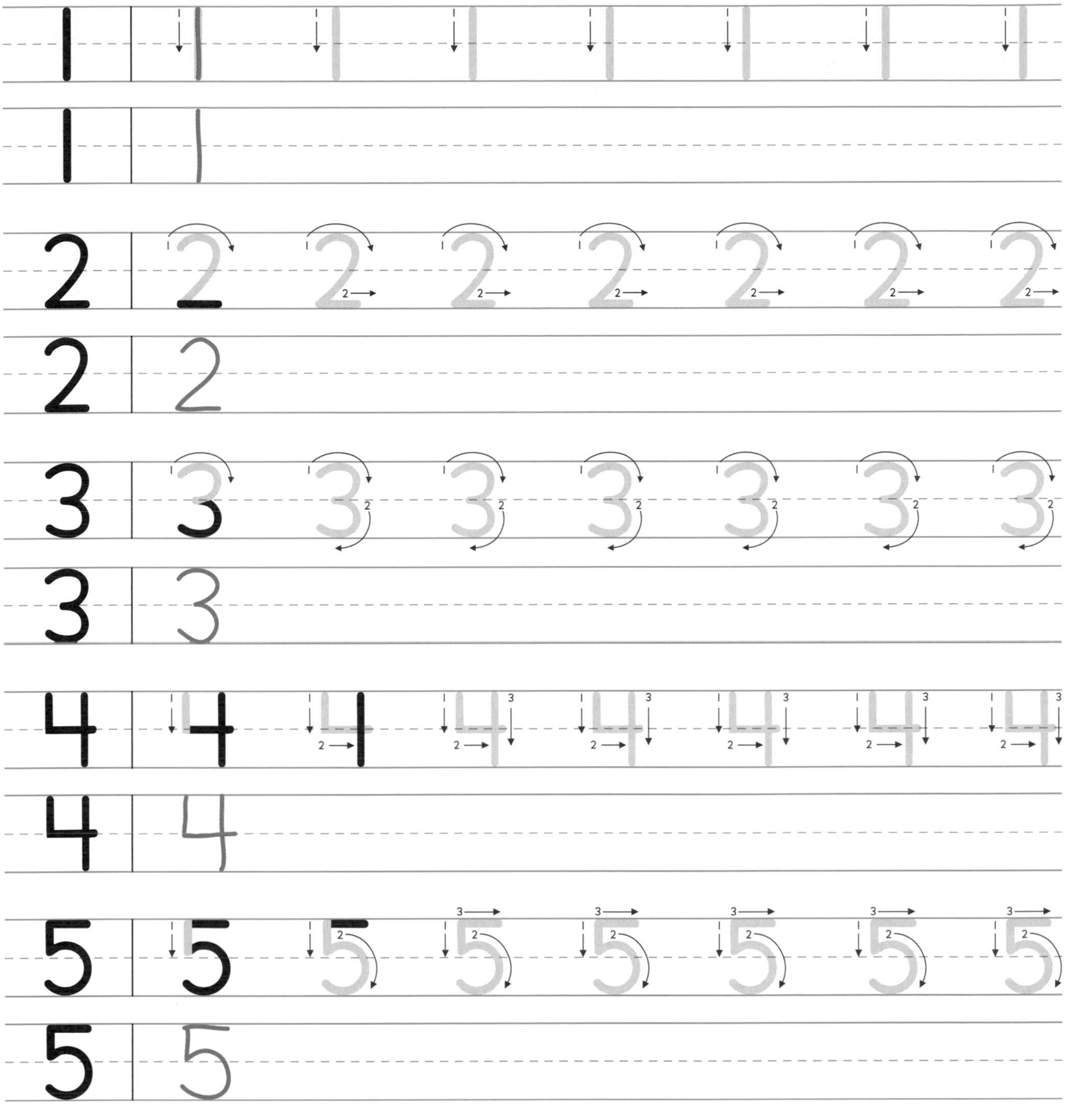

TEACHER

Literacy: Trace and write numerals 1–5, using left-to-right and top-to-bottom directionality in sequential strokes.
More practice: Worksheet 7 (Teacher's Edition CD-ROM).

Trace and write.

6 6 6 6 6 6 6

6 6

7 7 7 7 7 7 7

7 7

8 8 8 8 8 8 8

8 8

9 9 9 9 9 9 9

9 9

10 10 10 10 10 10 10

10 10

TEACHER

Literacy: Trace and write numerals 6–10, using left-to-right and top-to-bottom directionality in sequential strokes.
More practice: Worksheets 8–9 (Teacher's Edition CD-ROM).

🎧 Look and listen.

🎧 Listen again and repeat.

🎧 Listen. Circle the picture.

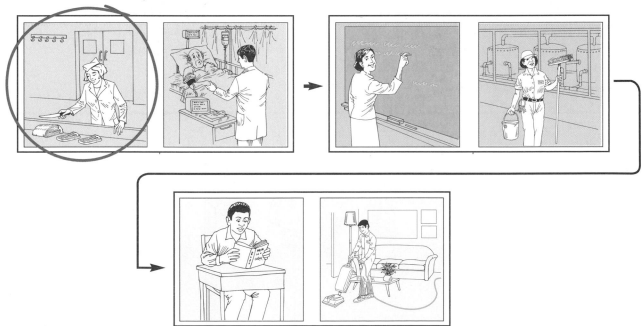

TEACHER

Survival: Learn names of some occupations.
Civics concept: Jobs are not determined by gender.
New language: Teacher, student, housecleaner, janitor, butcher, nurse.

🎧 **Look and listen.**

🎧 **Listen again and repeat.**

🎧 **Look and listen.**

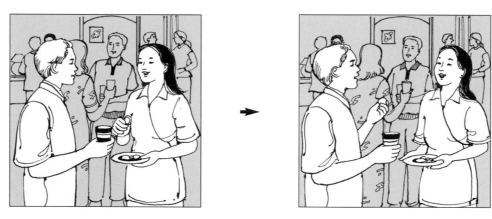

🎧 **Listen again and repeat.**

Pair work.

🎧 **Look and listen.**

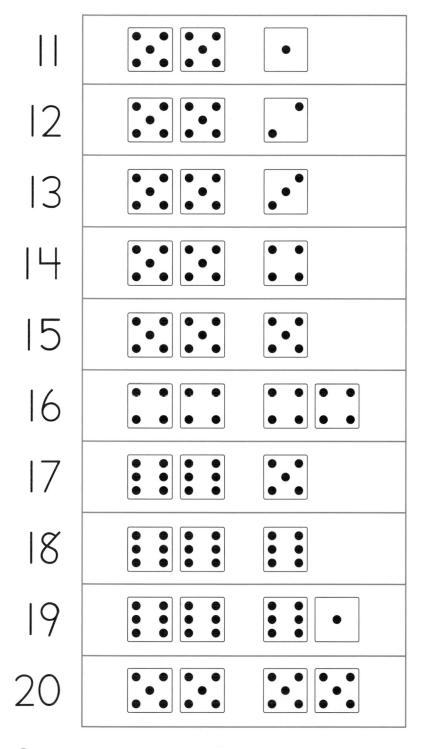

🎧 **Listen again and repeat.**

TEACHER

Literacy: Recognize numbers 11–20 and understand their meaning.

Trace.

11		11	11	11	11
12	2	12	12	12	12
13	3	13	13	13	13
14	4	14	14	14	14
15	5	15	15	15	15
16	6	16	16	16	16
17	7	17	17	17	17
18	8	18	18	18	18
19	9	19	19	19	19
20	20	20	20	20	20

TEACHER

Literacy: Trace numerals 11–20, using left-to-right and top-to-bottom directionality in sequential strokes.
More practice: Worksheet 10 (Teacher's Edition CD-ROM).

🎧 **Look and listen.**

🎧 **Listen again and repeat.**

Pair work.

TEACHER

Survival: Ask about another's state of health. Tell about one's own.
Civics concepts: It's polite to ask about another's health. It's important to say thanks when someone asks about your health.
New language: How are you? / Fine, thanks. / Great.

🎧 Listen. Circle the occupation.

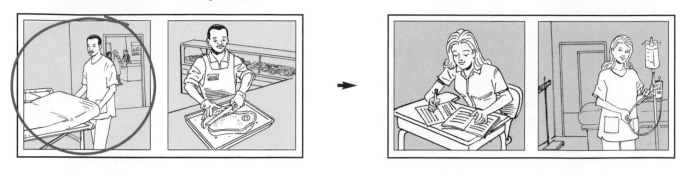

🎧 Look and listen.

🎧 Listen and respond.

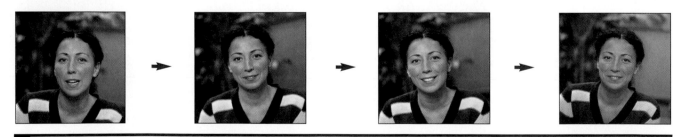

🎧 **Look and listen.**

21 ➔ 22 ➔ 23 ➔ 24 ➔ 25

26 ➔ 27 ➔ 28 ➔ 29 ➔ 30

APRIL						
S	M	T	W	T	F	S
	1	2	3	4	5	6
7	8	9	10	11	12	13
14	15	16	17	18	19	20
21	22	23	24	25	26	27
28	29	30				

🎧 **Listen again and repeat.**

Trace.

S	M	T	W	T	F	S
	1	2	3	4	5	6
7	8	9	10	11	12	13
14	15	16	17	18	19	20
21	22	23	24	25	26	27
28	29	30				

🎧 **Look and listen.**

31	32	33	34	35	36	37	38	39	40
41	42	43	44	45	46	47	48	49	50
51	52	53	54	55	56	57	58	59	60
61	62	63	64	65	66	67	68	69	70
71	72	73	74	75	76	77	78	79	80
81	82	83	84	85	86	87	88	89	90
91	92	93	94	95	96	97	98	99	100

🎧 **Listen again and repeat.**

Write.

31	32	33	34	35	36	37	38	39	40

41	42	43		45		47	48		50

71		73	74		76			79	80

91	92			95	96	97	98	99	

Talk about the picture. Role-play conversations.

TEACHER

Survival / civics review: Point and name things in the picture. Make sentences about the picture. Role-play conversations based on the picture.
Listening-speaking tests: Teacher's Edition CD-ROM.

Pair work.

56

12	8	23
75	64	100
98	47	11

Write.

11	12	13	14	15	16	17	18	-----	20

51	-----	-----	54	55	56	-----	-----	59	60

61	62	63	-----	65	66	67	68	-----	

81	82	-----	84	85	-----	-----	88	89	90

Write the numbers.

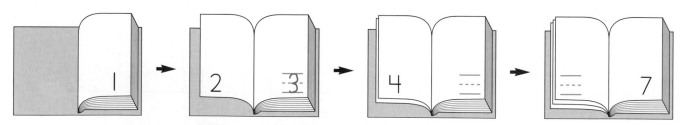

1 → 2 3 → 4 --- → --- 7

Literacy review: Understand, identify, say, and write numbers 1–100. Understand sequence of numbers. Understand that book pages are numbered in sequence.
More practice: Worksheet 13 (Teacher's Edition CD-ROM).
Tests: Teacher's Edition CD-ROM.

🎧 **Look and listen.**

1.

2.

3.

4.

5.

6.

7.

8.

🎧 **Listen again and repeat.**

🎧 **Listen. Circle the picture.**

1.

2.

3.

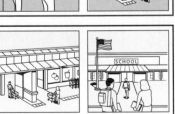

4.

5.

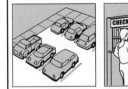

6.

TEACHER

Survival: Learn names for places in the community.
New language: Bus stop, station, bank, library, supermarket, school, post office, parking lot.

🎧 Look and listen.

1.

2.

🎧 Listen again and repeat.

Pair work.

NAME _____

🎧 **Look and listen.**

E   F

🎧 **Listen again and repeat.**

🎧 **Listen. Circle the letter.**

1. | E | F | 2. | E | F | 3. | E | F |

Cross out the letters.

E	E	E	E	✗	E
F	F	F	E	F	F
E	E	E	F	E	F
F	F	E	F	F	E

Trace and write.

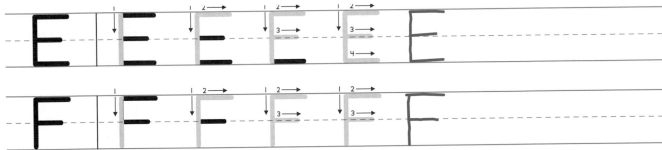

TEACHER

Literacy: Recognize, trace, and write capital letters E and F, using left-to-right and top-to-bottom directionality in sequential strokes; learn and say their "names."
More practice: Worksheet 14 (Teacher's Edition CD-ROM).

∩ Look and listen.

T   I   L

∩ Listen again and repeat.

Circle the letters.

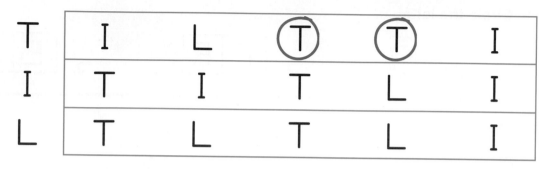

T	I	L	(T)	(T)	I
I	T	I	T	L	I
L	T	L	T	L	I

Trace and write.

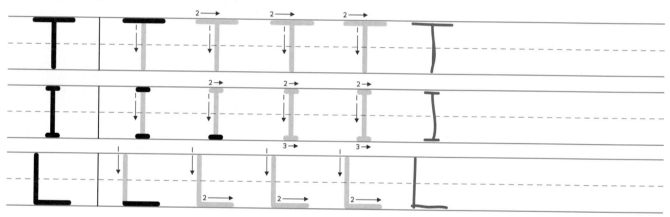

∩ Listen and write.

1.   2. _____ 3. _____ 4. _____ 5. _____

Say the names of the letters.

L   F   I   E   T

TEACHER

Literacy: Recognize, trace, and write capital letters T, I, and L, using left-to-right and top-to-bottom directionality in sequential strokes; learn and say their "names." Review E and F.
More practice: Worksheet 15 (Teacher's Edition CD-ROM).

🎧 Look and listen.

1.

2.

🎧 Listen again and repeat.

🎧 Look and listen.

 →

🎧 Listen again and repeat.

Pair work.

 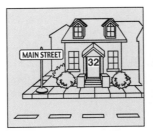  

🎧 Look and listen.

 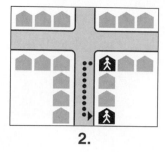 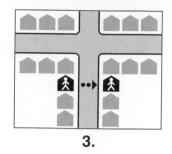

1.   2.   3.

🎧 Listen again and repeat.

🎧 Look and listen.

🎧 Listen again and repeat.

Pair work.

   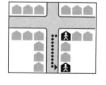 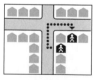

 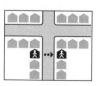

TEACHER

Survival: Ask for and give location and directions. Clarify what is said.
New language: Around the corner, down the street, across the street.

🎧 **Look and listen.**

 A   H   Y

🎧 **Listen again and repeat.**

Circle the letters.

A	H	Y	(A)	H	(A)
A	H	A	H	A	Y
H	A	H	A	Y	H
Y	H	H	Y	A	Y

Trace and write.

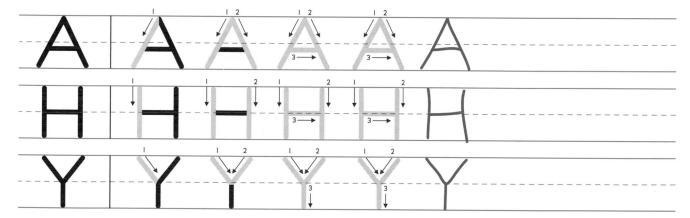

🎧 **Listen and write.**

1. H   2. _____   3. _____   4. _____   5. _____

🎧 **Look and listen.**

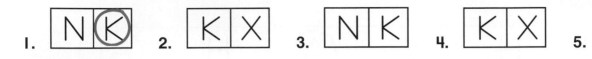

N   Z   K   X

🎧 **Listen again and repeat.**

🎧 **Listen. Circle the letter.**

1. | N | Ⓚ | 2. | K | X | 3. | N | K | 4. | K | X | 5. | N | Z |

Cross out the letters.

N	N	N	N	Z̶	X̶
Z	K	K	N	Z	Z
K	K	N	Z	K	X
X	Z	K	X	N	X

Trace and write.

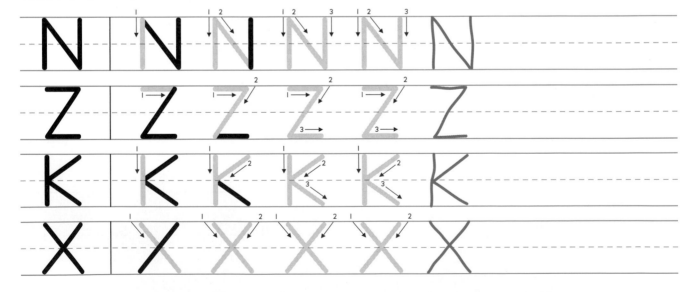

Literacy: Recognize, trace, and write capital letters N, Z, K, and X, using left-to-right and top-to-bottom directionality in sequential strokes; learn and say their "names."
More practice: Worksheet 17 (Teacher's Edition CD-ROM).

TEACHER

🎧 **Look and listen.**

TOM YU	TOM YU	TOM YU
45 MAIN STREET	45 MAIN STREET	45 MAIN STREET
MILLTOWN, NJ 07079	MILLTOWN, NJ 07079	MILLTOWN, NJ 07079
1.	**2.**	**3.**

🎧 **Listen again and repeat.**

🎧 **Listen. Circle the picture.**

1.

MARY DEE	MARY DEE
6201 AVENUE K	6201 AVENUE K
PIMA, TEXAS 78222	PIMA, TEXAS 78222

2.

MARY DEE	MARY DEE
6201 AVENUE K	6201 AVENUE K
PIMA, TEXAS 78222	PIMA, TEXAS 78222

3.

MARY DEE	MARY DEE
6201 AVENUE K	6201 AVENUE K
PIMA, TEXAS 78222	PIMA, TEXAS 78222

Say the zip codes.

1. 12573   2. 41586   3. 39001

🎧 **Listen. Write the zip code.**

1. 32421   2. _____   3. _____

🎧 **Look and listen.**

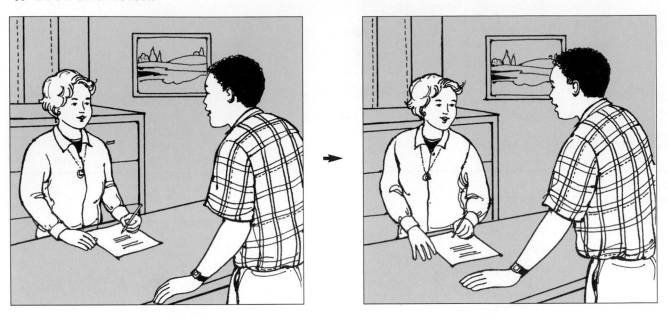

🎧 **Listen again and repeat.**

Pair work.

🎧 **Look and listen.**

M W V

🎧 **Listen again and repeat.**

Circle the letters.

M	V	V	Ⓜ	Ⓜ	W
M	W	V	M	W	M
V	M	V	W	V	M
W	V	M	W	V	M

Trace and write.

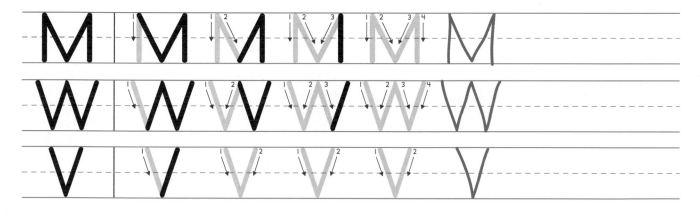

🎧 **Listen and write.**

1. V 2. _____ 3. _____ 4. _____

TEACHER

Literacy: Recognize, trace, and write capital letters M, W, and V, using left-to-right and top-to-bottom directionality in sequential strokes; learn and say their "names."
More practice: Worksheet 18 (Teacher's Edition CD-ROM).

🎧 **Look and listen.**

U   J   S

🎧 **Listen again and repeat.**

Cross out the the letters.

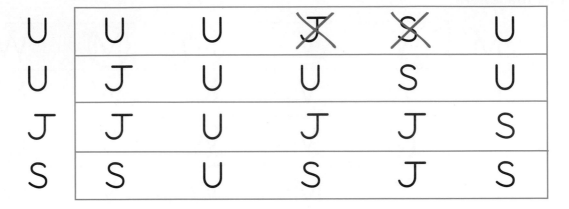

U	U	U	X̶	X̶	U
U	J	U	U	S	U
J	J	U	J	J	S
S	S	U	S	J	S

Trace and write.

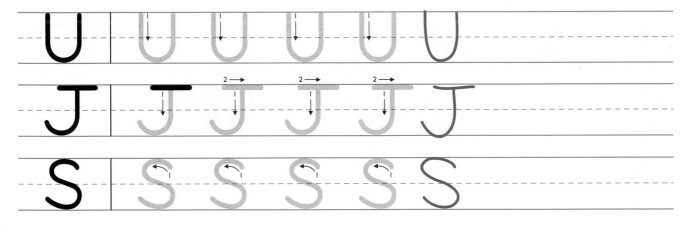

Say the names of the letters.

M   S   U   W   V   J

TEACHER

Literacy: Recognize, trace, and write U, J, and S; learn and say their "names." Review M, W, V.
More practice: Worksheet 19 (Teacher's Edition CD-ROM).

∩ Look and listen.

∩ Listen again and repeat.

Pair work.

TEACHER

Survival: Ask for directions to a street address. Ask for repetition.

Civics concept: House addresses are often numbered with odd numbers on one side of the street and even numbers on the other.

New language: I'm looking for [9 M Street]. / Could you repeat that, please? / Sure. / This is [number 10].

 **Listen and circle.**

1. [(22) | 2]   2. [87 | 78]   3. [16 | 61]

🎧 **Look and listen.**

 →

 →

🎧 **Listen and respond.**

1.   2.   3.   4.

🎧 Look and listen.

O   C   G   Q

🎧 Listen again and repeat.

🎧 Listen. Circle the letter.

1. G Q   2. O C   3. G Q   4. C G   5. Q G

Cross out the letters.

O	O	O	⨉	⨉	O
C	C	C	O	C	G
G	Q	G	G	O	G
Q	Q	G	Q	Q	Q

Trace and write.

O   O O O O   O

C   C C C C   C

G   G G G G   G

Q   Q Q Q Q   Q

🎧 **Look and listen.**

B   D   P   R

🎧 **Listen again and repeat.**

Cross out the letters.

B	B	D̶	B	R̶	B
D	D	B	D	R	D
P	P	P	P	R	P
R	P	R	P	P	B

Trace and write.

B B B B B B

D D D D D D

P P P P P P

R R R R R R

🎧 **Listen and write.**

1. D   2. ____   3. ____   4. ____   5. ____

TEACHER

Literacy: Recognize, trace, and write capital letters B, D, P, and R; learn and say their "names."
More practice: Worksheet 21 (Teacher's Edition CD-ROM).

Talk about the picture. Role-play conversations.

Trace and write.

Say the names of the letters.

A B C D E F G H I J K L M
N O P Q R S T U V W X Y Z

Literacy review: Trace, write, read, and say all the capital letters of the alphabet.
More practice: Worksheets 22–23 (Teacher's Edition CD-ROM).
Tests: Teacher's Edition CD-ROM.

🎧 **A. Look and listen.**

I.   2.   3.   4.

🎧 **B. Listen again and repeat.**

🎧 **C. Look and listen.**

I.   2.   3.   4.   5.

🎧 **D. Listen again and repeat.**

🎧 **E. Listen. Circle the picture.**

I.   2.   3.

  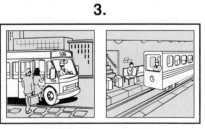

4.   5.   6.

🎧 A. Look and listen.

1.

2.

3.

4.

🎧 B. Listen again and repeat.

C. Pair work.

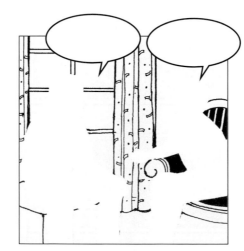

NAME ________________________

A. Look and listen.

A → B → C → D → E → F → G

H → I → J → K

L → M → N → O → P

Q → R → S

T → U → V

W → X

Y → Z

B. Listen again and repeat.

C. Write your name. Say the letters.

NAME ________________________

TEACHER

Literacy: See letters in alphabetical order. Hear "names" of letters in a chant. Repeat names of letters after the chant. Write one's own name and say the letters.
More practice: Worksheet 24 (Teacher's Edition CD-ROM).

🎧 **A. Listen and repeat.**

A B C
X Y Z
E F G
N O P
R S T
T U V
C D E

🎧 **B. Listen and repeat.**

1. A J K

2. B C D   E G P   T V Z

3. F L M   N S X

4. A H

C. Write your name. Spell your name for your partner.

A. Look and listen.

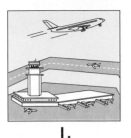
I.

2.

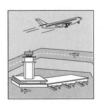
3.

4.

B. Listen again and repeat.

C. Look and listen.

I.

2.

D. Listen again and repeat.

E. Pair work.

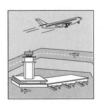

Survival: Get information about public transportation.
Civics concept: Buses and subway lines are identified by numbers, words, names, or letters.
New language: Airport, hospital, stadium, bridge / Which [bus] goes to the [hospital]? / The [3].

🎧 A. Look and listen.

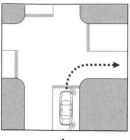

1.

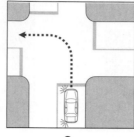

2.

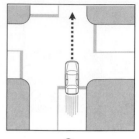

3.

🎧 B. Listen again and repeat.

🎧 C. Look and listen.

1.

2.

3.

🎧 D. Listen again and repeat.

E. Pair work.

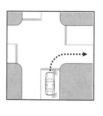

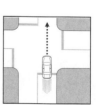

TEACHER

Survival: Ask for and give driving directions to a place.
Civics concept: It's OK to ask police for directions.
New language: Turn [right, left] at the corner. / Go straight.

50 • UNIT 3

A. Look at the letters.

Aa   Bb   Cc   Dd   Ee   Ff   Gg   Hh   Ii

Jj   Kk   Ll   Mm   Nn   Oo   Pp   Qq   Rr

Ss   Tt   Uu   Vv   Ww   Xx   Yy   Zz

B. Trace and write.

Vv   v   v   v   v   v

Ww   w   w   w   w   w

Xx   x   x   x   x   x

Zz   z   z   z   z   z

Ss   s   s   s   s   s

Oo   o   o   o   o   o

Cc   c   c   c   c   c

C. Look at the letters.

Vv   Ww   Xx   Zz   Ss   Oo   Cc

TEACHER

Literacy: Recognize, trace, and write lowercase letters with no descenders or ascenders, beginning with those that are the same as their capital forms (v, w, x, z, s, o, c). See serif versions of same letters, to prepare for reading.

More practice: Worksheets 25–26 (Teacher's Edition CD-ROM).

A. Trace and write.

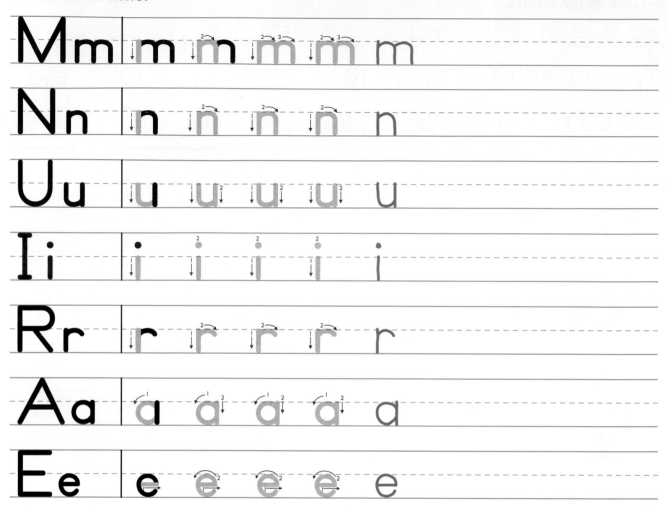

B. Look at the letters.

| Mm | Nn | Uu | Ii | Rr | Aa | Ee |

TEACHER

Literacy: Recognize, trace, and write lowercase letters with no descenders or ascenders (m, n, u, i, r, a, e). See serif versions of same letters, to prepare for reading.
More practice: Worksheets 27–28 (Teacher's Edition CD-ROM).

 **A. Look and listen.**

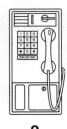

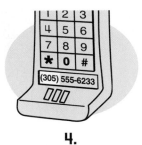

1.   2.   3.   4.

B. Listen again and repeat.

C. Look and listen.

 →

D. Listen again and repeat.

E. Pair work.

A. Look and listen.

1.

666-3211

2.

523-7904

3.

LISA
(915) 555-0456

4.

JOHN
?

B. Listen again and repeat.

C. Pair work.

433-6788

(801) 222-5466

?

TEACHER

Survival: Ask someone to make a phone call. Use "please" for polite requests.
Civics concept: You need an area code for calls outside of your own area code.
New language: Call [me], please. / What's the number? / I don't know.

A. Trace and write.

NAME _____

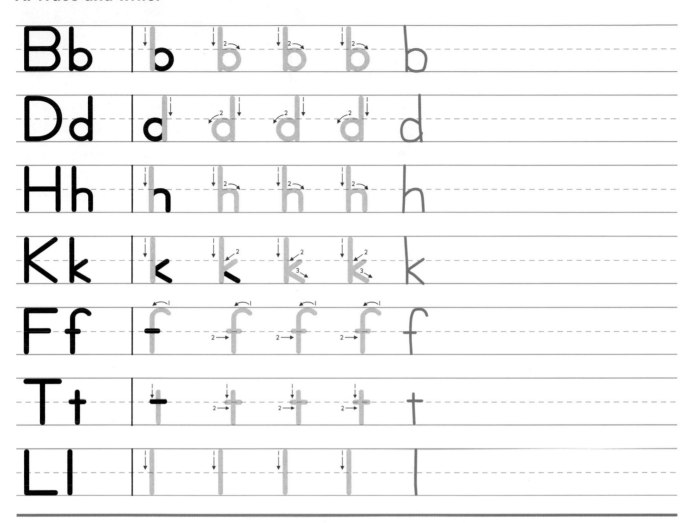

B. Look at the letters.

Bb   Dd   Hh   Kk   Ff   Tt   Ll

TEACHER

Literacy: Recognize, trace, and write lowercase letters with ascenders (b, d, h, k, f, t, l). See serif versions of same letters, to prepare for reading.
More practice: Worksheets 29–30 (Teacher's Edition CD-ROM).

A. Trace and write.

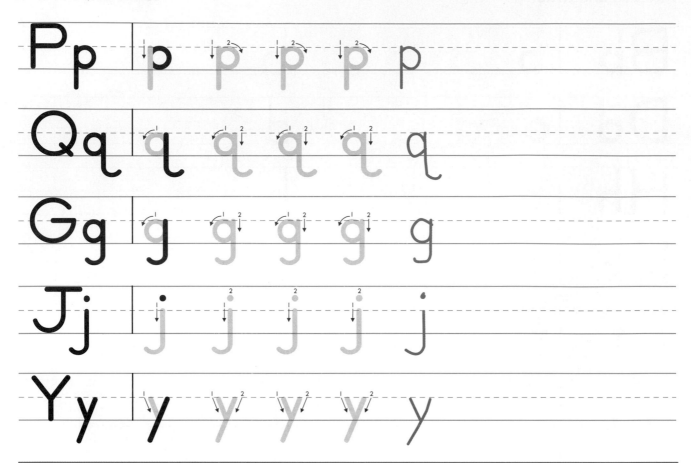

B. Match the letters.

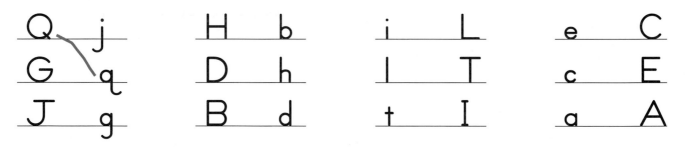

Q	j		H	b		i	L		e	C
G	q		D	h		l	T		c	E
J	g		B	d		t	I		a	A

C. Look at the letters.

Pp   Qq   Gg   Jj   Yy

TEACHER

Literacy: Recognize, trace, and write lowercase letters with descenders (p, q, g, j, y). Practice visually discriminating similar forms. See serif versions of same letters, to prepare for reading.
More practice: Worksheets 31–32 (Teacher's Edition CD-ROM).

🎧 A. Look and listen.

🎧 B. Listen again and repeat.

🎧 C. Look and listen.

🎧 D. Listen again and repeat.

E. Pair work.

TEACHER

Survival: Get public transportation directions on the phone. Ask for clarification.
Civics concept: Stops on public transportation are named by places you get on and get off.
New language: I need directions. / Are you taking the [bus]? / Take the [5] to [Main Street].

🎧 A. Listen and circle.

 1.  2. 3.
| Manne | Mann |

🎧 B. Look and listen.

 →

 →

🎧 C. Listen and respond.

 1.  2.  3.

TEACHER

Authentic practice: Students listen to an authentic conversation about name, address, and phone number and then complete listening and speaking tasks, providing true information about themselves.

NAME _____

A. Match the letters.

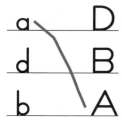 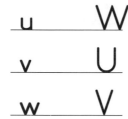 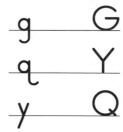 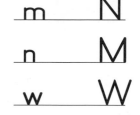

a	D		u	W		g	G		m	N
d	B		v	U		q	Y		n	M
b	A		w	V		y	Q		w	W

B. Look at the names.

first name

last name

first name

last name

C. Write your name.

_____
- - - - - - - - - - - - - - -
_____

first name

_____
- - - - - - - - - - - - - - -
_____

last name

TEACHER

Literacy: Write one's name as if on a form, using an initial capital letter.
More practice: Worksheet 33 (Teacher's Edition CD-ROM).

🎧 **A. Look and listen.**

<u>305</u>   <u>555-3248</u>
(area code)   phone number

🎧 **B. Listen. Write the telephone numbers.**

1. | 2 | 1 | 3 | | 5 | 5 | 5 | – | 4 | 5 | 2 | 1 |
(area code)   phone number

2. | | | | | | | | – | | | |
(area code)   phone number

3. | | | | | | | | – | | | |
(area code)   phone number

C. Write <u>your</u> name. Write your telephone number.

Peter   Macy   914 238-5803
first name   last name   (area code) telephone number

_____   _____   _____

first name   **last name**   **(area code)** **phone number**

TEACHER

Literacy: Fill out a form with both names, written in capital and lowercase letters, as well as area code and phone number.
More practice: Worksheet 34 (Teacher's Edition CD-ROM).

Talk about the pictures. Role-play conversations.

Survival / civics review: Point and name things in the pictures. Make sentences about the
pictures. Role-play conversations based on the pictures.
Listening-speaking tests: Teacher's Edition CD-ROM.

TEACHER

UNIT 3 • 61

A. Write the missing letters.

A B C D E F G

H I J ___ L M ___

___ P ___ ___ S U

W ___ ___ Z

a b c d e ___ g

___ i j ___ m

___ p r t ___

v ___ x ___ z

B. Write the numbers.

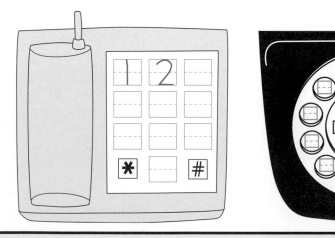

TEACHER

Literacy review: Capital and lowercase letters. Understand touch pad and rotary telephone dials.
More practice: Worksheets 35–36 (Teacher's Edition CD-ROM).
Tests: Teacher's Edition CD-ROM.

🎧 A. Look and listen.

   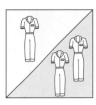  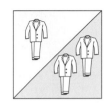

1.　　　2.　　　3.　　　4.　　　5.　　　6.

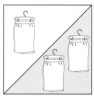  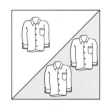 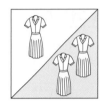 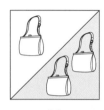

7.　　　8.　　　9.　　　10.　　　11.

🎧 B. Listen again and repeat.

🎧 C. Look and listen.

1.　　　2.　　　3.

🎧 D. Listen again and repeat.

🎧 E. Listen. Circle the picture.

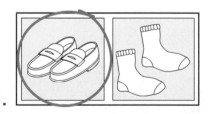   

1.　　　2.　　　3.

TEACHER

Survival: Learn vocabulary for types of clothing.
New language: Shoe[s], tie[s], robe[s], uniform[s], sock[s], suit[s], skirt[s], coat[s], shirt[s], dress[es], purse[s], pants, overalls, stockings.

A. Look and listen.

1.

2.

3.

B. Listen again and repeat.

C. Pair work.

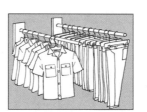

A. Look.

A*a*   B*b*   C*c*   D*d*   E*e*   F*f*   G*g*

H*h*   I*i*   J*j*   K*k*   L*l*   M*m*   N*n*

O*o*   P*p*   Q*q*   R*r*   S*s*   T*t*   U*u*

V*v*   W*w*   X*x*   Y*y*   Z*z*

B. Match the letters.

B C	O Q	T S	X N
C K	Q P	V U	H X
K B	R O	U V	M H
W W	P R	S T	N M

A D	G I	Y Z
D E	J J	Z Y
F A	I G	
E F	L L	

TEACHER

Literacy: Recognize capital letters in cursive.
More practice: Worksheet 37 (Teacher's Edition CD-ROM).

A. Look.

a a   b b   c c   d d   e e   f f   g g

h h   i i   j j   k k   l l   m m   n n

o o   p p   q q   r r   s s   t t   u u

v v   w w   x x   y y   z z

B. Match the letters.

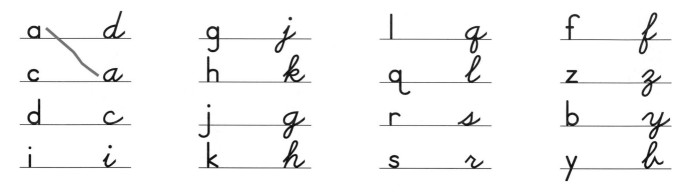

C. Trace your signature.

_____

signature

D. Sign your name.

_____

signature

TEACHER

Literacy: Recognize lowercase letters in cursive. Sign one's own name.
More practice: Worksheet 38 (Teacher's Edition CD-ROM).

🎧 A. Look and listen.

1. small   **2.** medium   **3.** large   **4.** extra large

🎧 B. Listen again and repeat.

🎧 C. Look and listen.

1.   **2.**   **3.**   **4.**

🎧 D. Listen again and repeat.

🎧 E. Listen and write.

 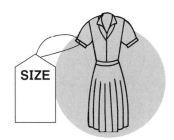

1.   **2.**

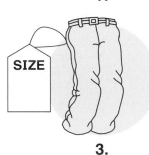 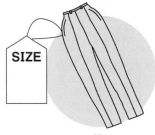

3.   **4.**

🎧 A. Look and listen.

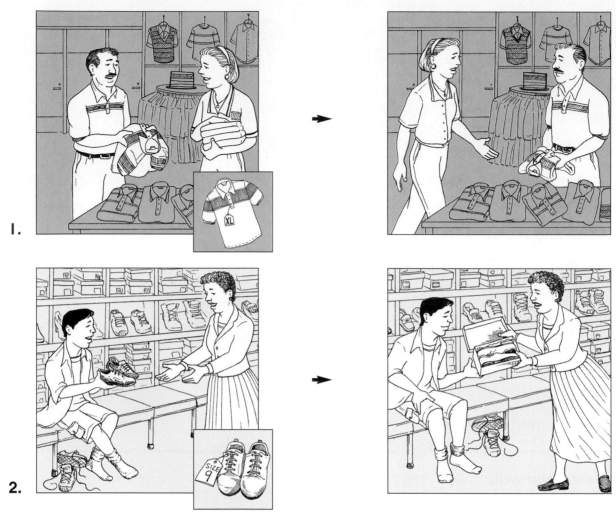

I.

2.

🎧 B. Listen again and repeat.

C. Pair work.

TEACHER

Survival: Ask for a size. Apologize.
Civics concept: Salespeople expect to get items in sizes that customers can't get for themselves.
New language: Do you have this [these] in [medium] [size 9]? / Just a minute. I'll check. / I'm
   sorry. We don't. / Here you go.

🎧 **A. Look at the letter s. Listen.**

s   small

🎧 **B. Listen again and repeat.**

🎧 **C. Look and listen.**

 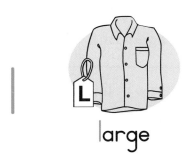

m   medium   l   large

🎧 **D. Listen again and repeat.**

🎧 **E. Listen. Circle the letter.**

1. (s) l l   2. m s   3. m l l   4. s l l

🎧 **F. Look and listen.**

  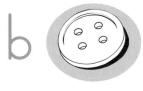 

t   tie   c   collar   b   button   p   pants

🎧 **G. Listen again and repeat.**

🎧 **H. Listen. Circle the letter.**

1. (t) l p   2. t l b   3. c l b   4. t l p

TEACHER

Literacy: Recognize the concept of initial consonant sound-symbol correspondence: s, m, l, t, c, b, p.
More practice: Worksheet 39 (Teacher's Edition CD-ROM).

🎧 **A. Look and listen.**

v   k   z

vest   key   zipper

🎧 **B. Listen again and repeat.**

🎧 **C. Listen. Circle the letter.**

1. v (z)   2. k z   3. v z

D. Trace the letters.

1. medium   2. library   3. parking lot

4. suit   5. bus   6. taxi   7. car

🎧 A. Look and listen.

1. a shoe store

2. a drugstore

3. a deli

4. a laundromat

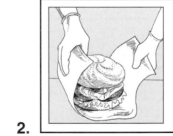

5. a gas station

6. a restaurant

🎧 B. Listen again and repeat.

🎧 C. Listen. Circle the picture.

1.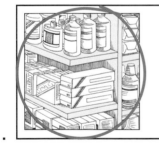

2.

3.

4.

TEACHER

Survival: Learn names of stores and other places to acquire service.
Civics concept: Know where to go to get particular goods and services.
New language: A shoe store, a drugstore, a deli, a laundromat, a gas station, a restaurant.

 **A. Look and listen.**

1. a salesperson   2. a customer   3. a cashier   4. a manager

B. Listen again and repeat.

C. Look and listen.

D. Listen again and repeat.

E. Pair work.

🎧 **A. Look and listen.**

d

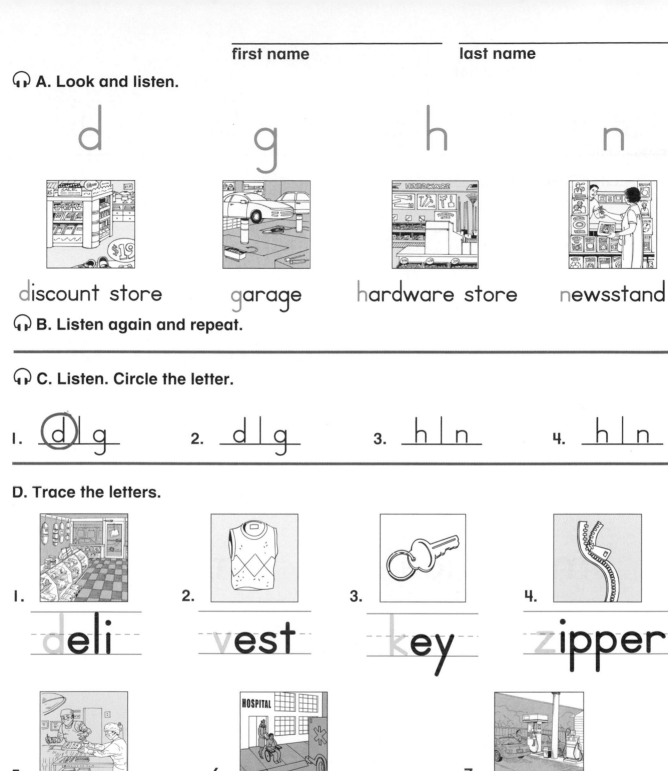

discount store   garage   hardware store   newsstand

🎧 **B. Listen again and repeat.**

🎧 **C. Listen. Circle the letter.**

1. ⓓ l g   2. d l g   3. h l n   4. h l n

D. Trace the letters.

1. deli   2. vest   3. key   4. zipper

5. nurse   6. hospital   7. gas station

TEACHER

Literacy: Recognize initial consonants d, g, h. n. Trace initial consonants at beginning of known words.
More practice: Worksheet 41 (Teacher's Edition CD-ROM).

🎧 A. Listen. Circle the letter.

1. (d) l g   2. d l g   3. h l n   4. h l n

🎧 B. Listen. Trace the letters.

1. deli   2. drive   3. dress

4. go   5. garage   6. gas station

7. hi   8. how   9. housecleaner

10. name   11. nice   12. number

 **A. Look and listen.**

B. Listen again and repeat.

C. Pair work.

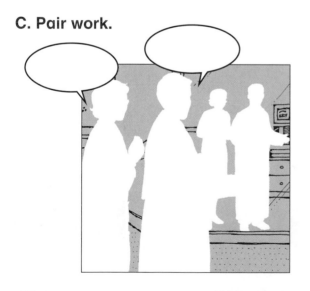

TEACHER

Survival: Comment on size.

Civics concept: Customers are entitled to satisfaction in a retail store.

New language: How is it? / It's too small [too large, fine]. / I'll take it.

🎧 A. Listen. Circle the picture.

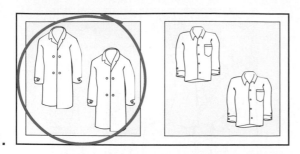

1.

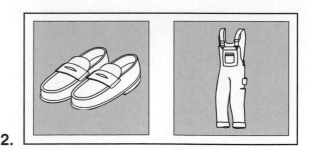

2.

3.

🎧 B. Look and listen.

🎧 C. Listen and respond.

1.

2.

3.

A. Look and listen.

j

jacket

r

raincoat

w

watch

B. Listen again and repeat.

C. Listen. Circle the letter.

1. j | w   2. j | r   3. r | j   4. r | w

D. Trace the letters.

1.

jacket

2.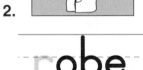
robe

3.
walk

TEACHER

Literacy: Recognize initial consonants j, r, w and trace them at beginning of known words.

🎧 **A. Look and listen.**

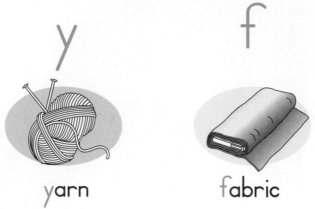

yarn   fabric

🎧 **B. Listen again and repeat.**

🎧 **C. Listen. Circle the letter.**

1. (y) | f   2. y | f   3. y | f   4. y | f

🎧 **D. Listen. Trace the letters.**

1. janitor   2. right   3. walk

4. with   5. yes   6. your

7. ferry   8. first name

Talk about the picture. Role-play conversations.

TEACHER

Survival / civics review: Point and name things in the picture. Make sentences about the picture. Role-play conversations based on the picture.
Listening-speaking tests: Teacher's Edition CD-ROM.

A. Match the letters.

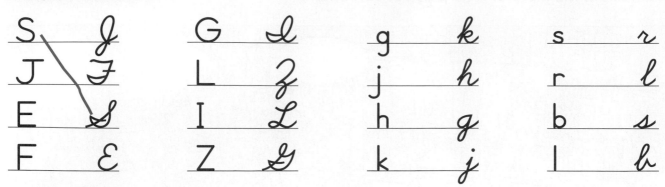

S $\mathcal{J}$ G $\mathcal{L}$ g   k   s z

J $\mathcal{F}$ L $\mathcal{Z}$ j   h   r l

E $\mathcal{S}$ I $\mathcal{L}$ h g b   s

F $\mathcal{E}$ Z $\mathcal{G}$ k j l h

B. Sign your name.

_____

signature

C. Trace.

button   yarn   fabric   zipper   watch

tie   collar   deli   garage   jacket

vest   pants   key   small   large

TEACHER

Literacy review: Review recognition of cursive capital and lowercase letters; sign one's own name in cursive capital and lowercase letters; recognize sound-symbol correspondence and trace initial consonants of known words.

More practice: Worksheets 43–44 (Teacher's Edition CD-ROM).

Tests: Teacher's Edition CD-ROM.

🎧 **A. Look and listen.**

7:00	12:00	5:10	11:48
1.	2.	3.	4.

🎧 **B. Listen again and repeat.**

🎧 **C. Look and listen.**

1.

2.

3.

🎧 **D. Listen again and repeat.**

E. Pair work.

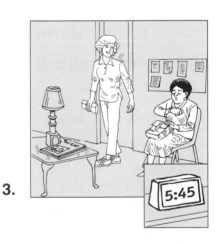

TEACHER

Survival: Tell time. Ask someone for the time.
Civics concept: It's OK to ask strangers for the time.
New language: What time is it? / It's [9:00].

A. Look and listen.

1. get up

2. eat

3. go to work

4. go home

5. watch TV

6. go to sleep

B. Listen again and repeat.

C. Look and listen.

1.

2.

3.

D. Listen again and repeat.

E. Pair work.

8:00   8:55   6:05

	first name	last name

A. Look and listen.

a

hat

rat

e

ten

pen

i

pit

mitt

o

hot

pot

u

sun

bun

B. Listen again and repeat.

C. Listen. Circle the sound.

1. u (e) 2. i l o 3. u l a 4. e l i 5. u l i

TEACHER

Literacy: Recognize sound-symbol correspondence of the short vowel sounds in minimal pairs. Learn the meaning of the words.
More practice: Worksheet 45 (Teacher's Edition CD-ROM).

UNIT 5 • 83

Read and say the words.

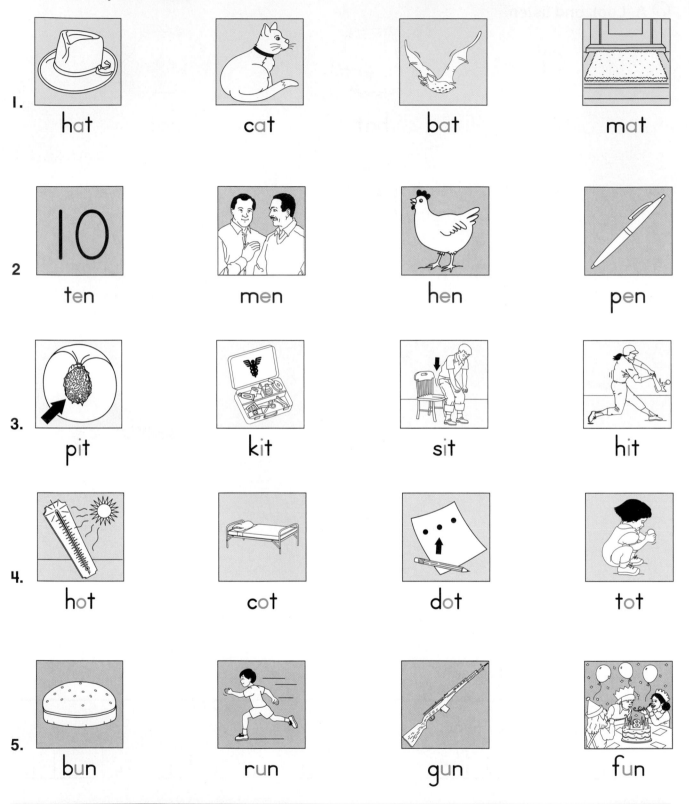

1.	hat	cat	bat	mat
2	ten	men	hen	pen
3.	pit	kit	sit	hit
4.	hot	cot	dot	tot
5.	bun	run	gun	fun

TEACHER

Literacy: Read one-syllable short-vowel words that have the same spelling / rhyming pattern. Learn the meaning of the words.
More practice: Worksheet 46 (Teacher's Edition CD-ROM).

84 • UNIT 5

🎧 A. Look and listen.

	MAY					
S	M	T	W	T	F	S
				1	2	3
4	5	6	7	8	9	10
11	12	13	14	15	16	17
18	19	20	21	22	23	24
25	26	27	28	29	30	31

1. a month

	MAY					
S	M	T	W	T	F	S
				1	2	3
4	5	6	7	8	9	10
11	12	13	14	15	16	17
18	19	20	21	22	23	24
25	26	27	28	29	30	31

2. a week

	MAY					
S	M	T	W	T	F	S
				1	2	3
4	5	6	7	8	9	10
11	12	13	14	15	16	17
18	19	20	21	22	23	24
25	26	27	28	29	30	31

3. a day

2004

JANUARY	FEBRUARY	MARCH	APRIL	MAY	JUNE

JULY	AUGUST	SEPTEMBER	OCTOBER	NOVEMBER	DECEMBER

4. a year

🎧 B. Listen again and repeat.

🎧 C. Look and listen.

JUNE						
Sunday	Monday	Tuesday	Wednesday	Thursday	Friday	Saturday

🎧 D. Listen again and repeat.

🎧 E. Look and listen.

 →

🎧 F. Listen again and repeat.

TEACHER

Survival: Ask about daily schedules.

Civics concepts: Work and school times are regular scheduled events. The months and the days have names.

New language: A month, a week, a day, a year / [Days of the week] / When do you [go to school]? / From [Monday] to [Friday]. / On [Wednesday].

A. Look and listen.

Nan Pitt

WORK SCHEDULE

MONDAY   9:00–5:00

B. Listen again and repeat.

C. Listen and circle.

1.

WORK SCHEDULE

MONDAY	9:00–5:00
TUESDAY	9:00–3:00
WEDNESDAY	9:00–5:00
THURSDAY	9:00–3:00
FRIDAY	9:00–12:00

2.

WORK SCHEDULE

MONDAY	12:00–5:00
TUESDAY	10:00–6:00
WEDNESDAY	10:00–6:00
THURSDAY	10:00–6:00
FRIDAY	9:00–12:00

3.

WORK SCHEDULE

MONDAY	———
TUESDAY	9:00–5:00
WEDNESDAY	9:00–5:00
THURSDAY	———
FRIDAY	9:00–12:00

D. Pair work.

WORK SCHEDULE

MONDAY	9:00–5:00
TUESDAY	9:00–3:00
WEDNESDAY	10:00–4:00
THURSDAY	9:00–5:00
FRIDAY	9:00–5:00

TEACHER

Survival: Discuss schedules and spans of time.
Civics concept: Be aware of work schedules.
New language: What are your work hours on [Monday]? / On [Monday], I work from [9] to [5].

🎧 **A. Look and listen.**

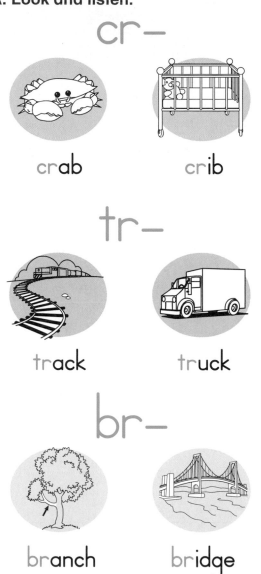

cr–

crab   crib

tr–

track   truck

br–

branch   bridge

dr–

dress   drip

fr–

frog   fridge

🎧 **B. Listen again and repeat.**

🎧 **C. Listen. Circle the letters.**

1. (tra) tru   2. fri | fro   3. dre | dru   4. bru | bri   5. cro | cri

TEACHER

Literacy: Recognize short vowel sounds when following initial consonant blends cr, dr, tr, fr, br.
More practice: Worksheet 47 (Teacher's Edition CD-ROM).

Trace and write.

1. dress   dress

2. drum   um

3. trap   ap

4. brick   ick

5. bridge   idge

6. fridge   idge

7. crop   op

8. crab   ab

Literacy: Trace and write words with initial consonant blends tr, fr, dr, br, cr and short vowels.
More practice: Worksheet 48 (Teacher's Edition CD-ROM).

A. Look and listen.

WORK SCHEDULE	
MONDAY	work 9:00
TUESDAY	work 8:00
WEDNESDAY	
THURSDAY	
FRIDAY	work 8:00

B. Listen again and repeat.

C. Pair work.

JANUARY								FEBRUARY								MARCH								APRIL								MAY								JUNE						
S	M	T	W	T	F	S		S	M	T	W	T	F	S		S	M	T	W	T	F	S		S	M	T	W	T	F	S		S	M	T	W	T	F	S		S	M	T	W	T	F	S
			1	2	3	4								1								1					1	2	3	4	5							1	2	3		1	2	3	4	5	6	7
5	6	7	8	9	10	11		2	3	4	5	6	7	8		2	3	4	5	6	7	8		6	7	8	9	10	11	12		4	5	6	7	8	9	10		8	9	10	11	12	13	14

JULY								AUGUST								SEPTEMBER								OCTOBER								NOVEMBER								DECEMBER						
S	M	T	W	T	F	S		S	M	T	W	T	F	S		S	M	T	W	T	F	S		S	M	T	W	T	F	S		S	M	T	W	T	F	S		S	M	T	W	T	F	S
		1	2	3	4	5							1	2		1	2	3	4	5	6				1	2	3	4								1		1	2	3	4	5	6
6	7	8	9	10	11	12		3	4	5	6	7	8	9		7	8	9	10	11	12	13		5	6	7	8	9	10	11		2	3	4	5	6	7	8		7	8	9	10	11	12	13

🎧 B. Listen again and repeat.

🎧 C. Look and listen.

1. It's hot.   2. It's warm.   3. It's cold.   4. It's cool.

🎧 D. Listen again and repeat.

🎧 E. Look and listen.

   →

🎧 F. Listen again and repeat.

G. Pair work.

JANUARY						
S	M	T	W	T	F	S
				1	2	3
4	5	6	7	8	9	10
11	12	13	14	15	16	17
18	19	20	21	22	23	24
25	26	27	28	29	30	31

AUGUST						
S	M	T	W	T	F	S
				1	2	3
4	5	6	7	8	9	10
11	12	13	14	15	16	17
18	19	20	21	22	23	24
25	26	27	28	29	30	31

TEACHER

Survival: Learn names of months and weather expressions. Ask about national origin.
Civics concept: Weather is a common topic in making friendly small talk.
New language: [Months of the year] / It's [hot, warm, cold, cool]. / Where are you from? / I'm from [France]. / What's the weather like there in [January]?

A. Look.

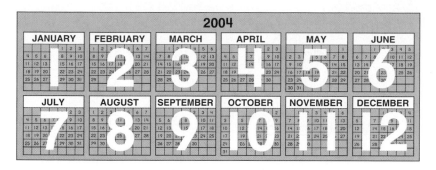

May 3, 2004 = 5/3/2004

B. Write the date with numbers.

JANUARY	2002					
S	M	T	W	T	F	S
		1	2	3	4	5
6	7	8	9	10	11	12
13	14	15	16	17	18	19
20	21	22	23	24	25	26
27	28	29	30	31		

AUGUST	1944					
S	M	T	W	T	F	S
		1	2	3	4	5
6	7	8	9	10	11	12
13	14	15	16	17	18	19
20	21	22	23	24	25	26
27	28	29	30	31		

DECEMBER	2003					
S	M	T	W	T	F	S
	1	2	3	4	5	6
7	8	9	10	11	12	13
14	15	16	17	18	19	20
21	22	23	24	25	26	27
28	29	30	31			

JUNE	2004					
S	M	T	W	T	F	S
		1	2	3	4	5
6	7	8	9	10	11	12
13	14	15	16	17	18	19
20	21	22	23	24	25	26
27	28	29	30			

1. 1/6/2002

2. _____

3. _____

4. _____

C. Look.

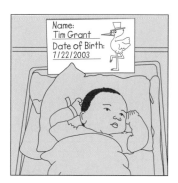

Name:
Tim Grant
Date of Birth:
7/22/2003

D. Write your date of birth in numbers.

date of birth: _____

TEACHER

Literacy: Write a date with numerals. Write one's own date of birth on a form, using numerals for the month, day, and year.
More practice: Worksheets 49–50 (Teacher's Edition CD-ROM).

UNIT 5 • 91

A. Match.

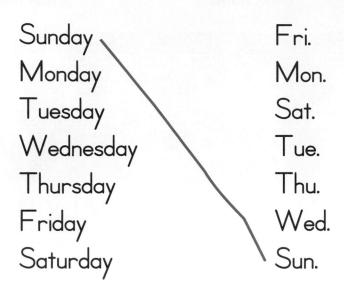

Sunday   Fri.
Monday   Mon.
Tuesday   Sat.
Wednesday   Tue.
Thursday   Thu.
Friday   Wed.
Saturday   Sun.

B. Circle.

1. January	(Jan.)	June
2. February	Sept.	Feb.
3. March	May	Mar.
4. August	Aug.	Apr.

C. Circle.

1. Oct.	December	(October)
2. Nov.	September	November
3. Dec.	November	December
4. Apr.	August	April
5. Sept.	September	October

Literacy: Understand concept of abbreviations and connect abbreviations with words for days of the week and months of the year.
More practice: Worksheet 51 (Teacher's Edition CD-ROM).

TEACHER

A. Look and listen.

1. morning 2. afternoon 3. evening 4. night

B. Listen again and repeat.

C. Look and listen.

1.

2.

3.

4.

D. Listen again and repeat.

E. Pair work.

A. Listen. Circle the picture.

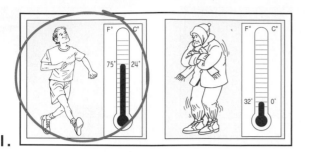

1.

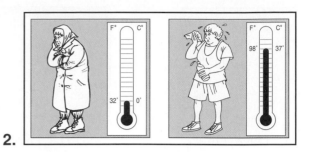

2.

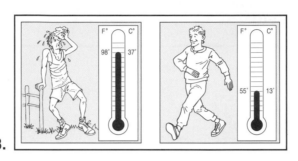

3.

B. Look and listen.

C. Listen and respond.

1.

2.

3.

first name _____ last name _____

🎧 **A. Look and listen.**

gl–

glass

sl–

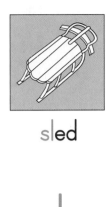

sled

cl–

clip

bl–

block

pl–

plum

🎧 **B. Listen again and repeat.**

🎧 **C. Listen. Circle the letters.**

1. slo (sle)   2. slo | sli   3. pli | plu   4. clo | cle   5. bla | blu

sk–

skin

sm–

smog

sp–

spot

st–

stop

sw–

swim

 B. Listen again and repeat.

 C. Listen. Circle the word.

1. spot (stop)

2. swim | skim

3. skin | spin

 D. Listen. Circle the letters.

1. (sk) sp

2. sm | sw

3. sp | st

4. sp | st

5. sw | sm

TEACHER

Literacy: Recognize initial consonant blends with s.
More practice: Worksheets 52–53 (Teacher's Edition CD-ROM).

Talk about the pictures. Role-play conversations.

TEACHER

Survival / civics review: Point and name things in the pictures. Make sentences about the pictures. Role-play conversations based on the pictures.
Listening-speaking tests: Teacher's Edition CD-ROM.

UNIT 5 • 97

A. Listen. Circle the time.

1. 6:50 / **6:15**
2. 5:25 / 5:00
3. 2:55 / 2:05
4. 1:30 / 3:10

B. Match.

January   February   June   July

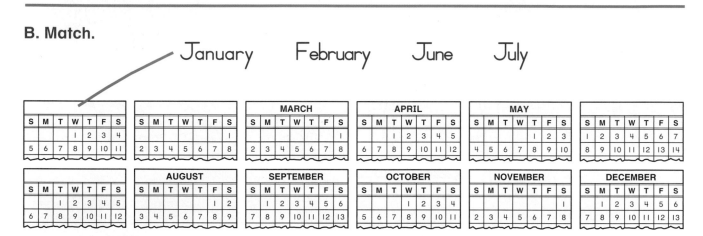

S	M	T	W	T	F	S
				1	2	3	4
5	6	7	8	9	10	11

S	M	T	W	T	F	S
						1
2	3	4	5	6	7	8

MARCH

S	M	T	W	T	F	S
						1
2	3	4	5	6	7	8

APRIL

S	M	T	W	T	F	S
		1	2	3	4	5
6	7	8	9	10	11	12

MAY

S	M	T	W	T	F	S
				1	2	3
4	5	6	7	8	9	10

S	M	T	W	T	F	S
1	2	3	4	5	6	7
8	9	10	11	12	13	14

S	M	T	W	T	F	S
	1	2	3	4	5	
6	7	8	9	10	11	12

AUGUST

S	M	T	W	T	F	S
					1	2
3	4	5	6	7	8	9

SEPTEMBER

S	M	T	W	T	F	S
	1	2	3	4	5	6
7	8	9	10	11	12	13

OCTOBER

S	M	T	W	T	F	S
		1	2	3	4	
5	6	7	8	9	10	11

NOVEMBER

S	M	T	W	T	F	S
						1
2	3	4	5	6	7	8

DECEMBER

S	M	T	W	T	F	S
	1	2	3	4	5	6
7	8	9	10	11	12	13

C. Write the date with numbers.

JANUARY 2002

S	M	T	W	T	F	S
		1	2	3	4	5
6	7	8	9	10	11	12
13	14	15	16	17	18	19
20	21	22	23	24	25	26
27	28	29	30	31		

JULY 1955

S	M	T	W	T	F	S
		1	2	3	4	5	6
7	8	9	10	11	12	13
14	15	16	17	18	19	20
21	22	23	24	25	26	27
28	29	30	31			

DECEMBER 2004

S	M	T	W	T	F	S
			1	2	3	4
5	6	7	8	9	10	11
12	13	14	15	16	17	18
19	20	21	22	23	24	25
26	27	28	29	30	31	

1. **1/10/2002**　　2. _____　　3. _____

D. Write your date of birth in numbers.

date of birth: _____

TEACHER

Literacy review: Review time telling, months of the year, and writing the date in numbers.
More practice: Worksheet 54 (Teacher's Edition CD-ROM).
Tests: Teacher's Edition CD-ROM.

🎧 **A. Look and listen.**

1. breakfast   2. lunch   3. dinner

🎧 **B. Listen again and repeat.**

🎧 **C. Listen. Circle the picture.**

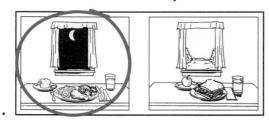   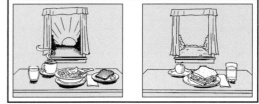

D. Match.

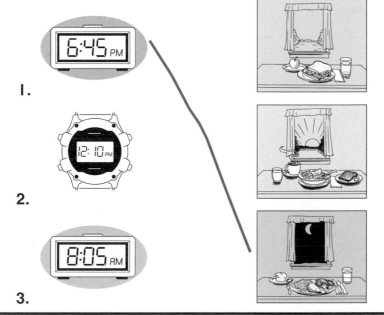

1.

2.

3.

TEACHER

Survival: Learn names of meals.
Civics concept: Recognize typical meal times of this culture.
New language: Breakfast, lunch, dinner, AM, PM.

🎧 A. Look and listen.

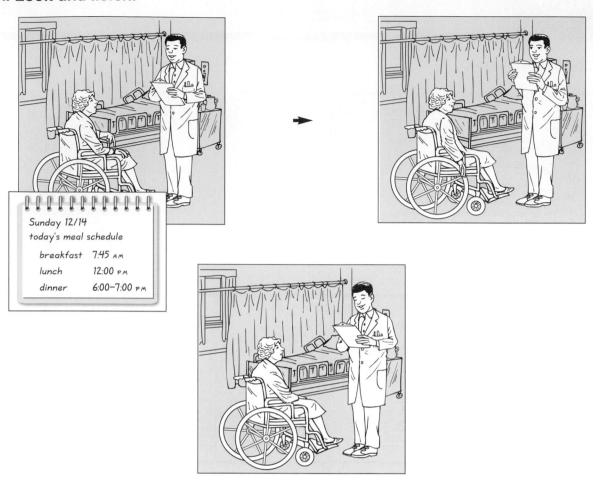

Sunday 12/14
today's meal schedule

breakfast	7:45 AM
lunch	12:00 PM
dinner	6:00–7:00 PM

🎧 B. Listen again and repeat.

C. Pair work.

meal schedule for today

breakfast	8:00–10:00 AM
lunch	noon
dinner	6:30 PM

first name   last name

🎧 A. Look and listen.

-g

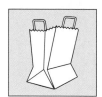
bag

rag

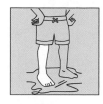
leg

peg

dig

pig

jog

log

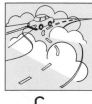
rug

mug

🎧 B. Listen again and repeat.

C. Read and say the words.

1. jog   2. pig   3. mug   4. rag   5. leg

D. Read and say the words.

fog

big

hug

wag

TEACHER

Literacy: Recognize sound-symbol correspondence of final consonant -g in one-syllable words with short vowels. Decode and say aloud corresponding sounds in new words.
More practice: Worksheet 55 (Teacher's Edition CD-ROM).

🎧 **A. Look and listen.**

–n

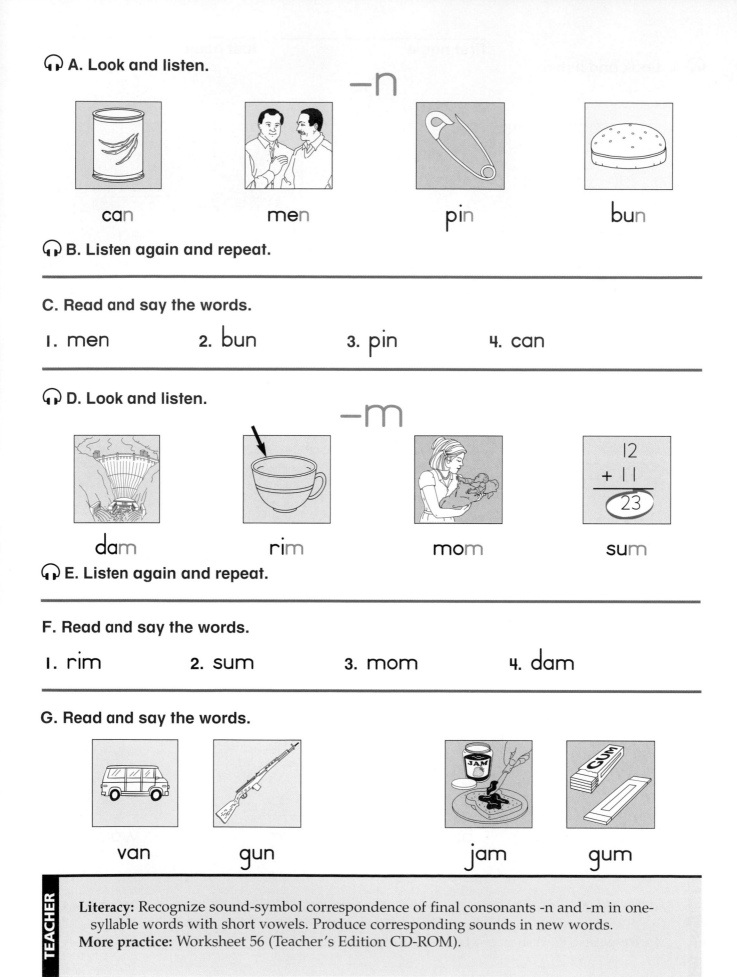

can   men   pin   bun

🎧 **B. Listen again and repeat.**

C. Read and say the words.

1. men   2. bun   3. pin   4. can

🎧 **D. Look and listen.**

–m

dam   rim   mom   sum

🎧 **E. Listen again and repeat.**

F. Read and say the words.

1. rim   2. sum   3. mom   4. dam

G. Read and say the words.

van   gun   jam   gum

🎧 A. Look and listen.

 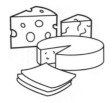   

1. fruit   2. cheese   3. meat   4. chicken   5. fish

6. rice   7. pasta   8. bread   9. cereal

🎧 B. Listen again and repeat.

🎧 C. Look and listen.

 ➡

🎧 D. Listen again and repeat.

E. Pair work.

TEACHER

Survival: Learn names of common foods.
New language: Fruit, cheese, meat, chicken, fish, rice, pasta, bread, cereal / What do you eat for [breakfast]? / I eat [cereal].

 **A. Look and listen.**

1. coffee

2. tea

3. milk

4. juice

5. water

6. sugar

7. salt

8. pepper

9. oil

10. butter

 **B. Listen again and repeat.**

C. Look and listen.

   →

D. Listen again and repeat.

E. Pair work.

A. Look and listen.

first name   last name

−b

         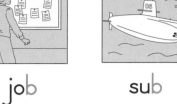

lab   web   job   sub

 B. Listen again and repeat.

C. Read and say the words.

1. sub   2. lab   3. job   4. web

D. Read and say the words.

cab   sob   tub

 E. Look and listen.

−s

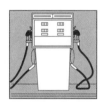

gas   bus

 F. Listen again and repeat.

G. Read and say the words.

1. bus   2. gas

TEACHER

Literacy: Recognize sound-symbol correspondence of final consonants -b and -s in one-syllable words with short vowels. Produce corresponding sounds in new words.
More practice: Worksheet 57 (Teacher's Edition CD-ROM).

🎧 **A. Look and listen.**

–p

 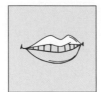 

map   lip   mop   cup

🎧 **B. Listen again and repeat.**

C. Read and say the words.

1. cup   2. lip   3. map   4. mop

🎧 **D. Look and listen.**

–x

  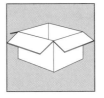 

fax   fix   box   tux

🎧 **E. Listen again and repeat.**

F. Read and say the words.

1. box   2. fix   3. fax   4. tux

G. Read and say the words.

cap   cop   wax   mix

TEACHER

Literacy: Recognize sound-symbol correspondence of final consonants -p and -x in one-syllable words with short vowels. Produce corresponding sounds in new words.
More practice: Worksheet 58 (Teacher's Edition CD-ROM).

🎧 A. Look and listen.

vegetables

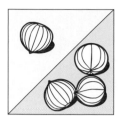 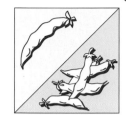 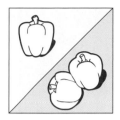 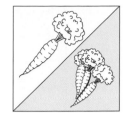

I. an onion/onions 2. a bean/beans 3. a pepper/peppers 4. a carrot/carrots

🎧 B. Listen again and repeat.

🎧 C. Look and listen.

fruits

 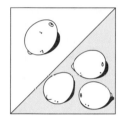  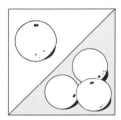

I. an apple/apples 2. a lemon/lemons 3. a banana/bananas 4. an orange/oranges

🎧 D. Listen again and repeat.

🎧 E. Listen. Circle the picture.

I. 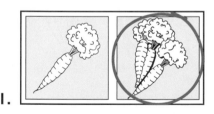   2.    3.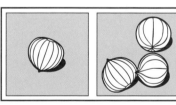

4.    5.     6.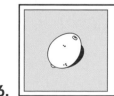

A. Look and listen.

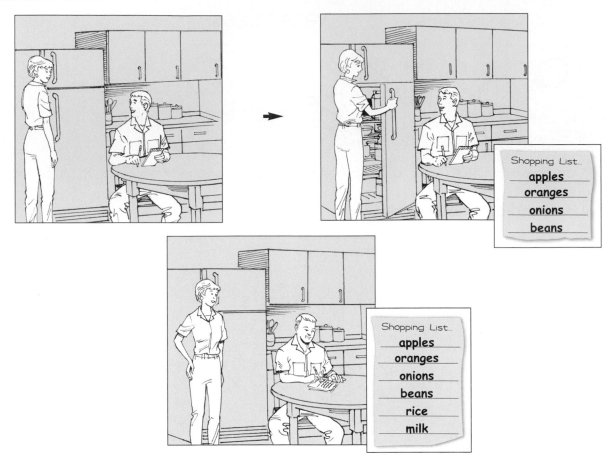

B. Listen again and repeat.

C. Pair work.

🎧 **A. Look and listen.**

–t

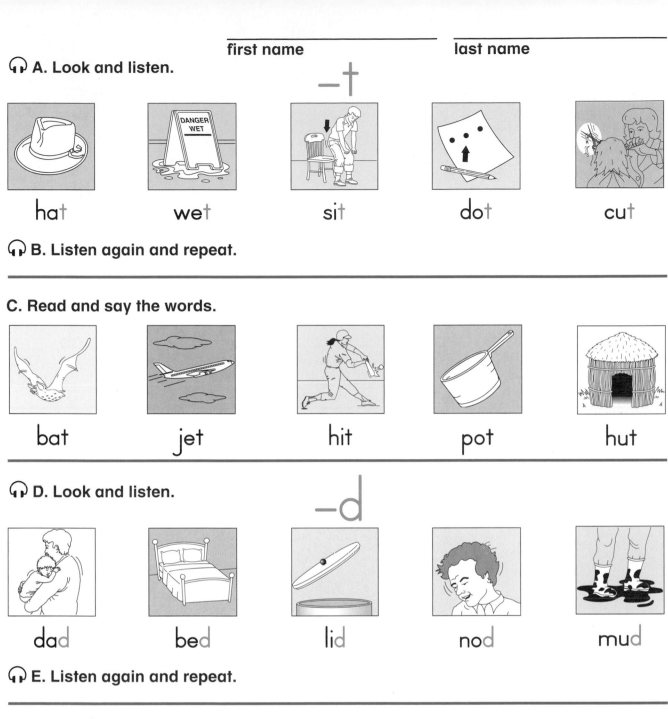

hat   wet   sit   dot   cut

🎧 **B. Listen again and repeat.**

C. Read and say the words.

bat   jet   hit   pot   hut

🎧 **D. Look and listen.**

–d

dad   bed   lid   nod   mud

🎧 **E. Listen again and repeat.**

F. Read and say the words.

sad   rod   bud

TEACHER

Literacy: Recognize sound-symbol correspondence of final consonants -t and -d in one-syllable words with short vowels. Produce corresponding sounds in new words.
More practice: Worksheet 59 (Teacher's Edition CD-ROM).

A. Look and listen.

plum

swim

clip

stop

frog

smog

crib

crab

B. Listen again and repeat.

C. Read and say the words.

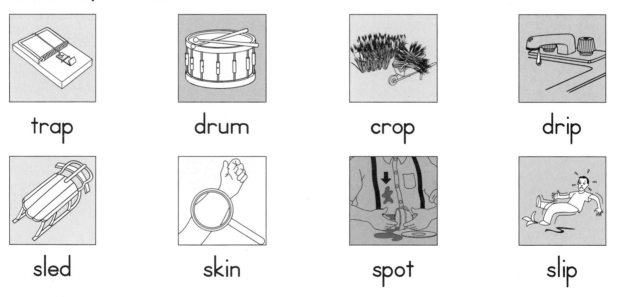

trap

drum

crop

drip

sled

skin

spot

slip

A. Look and listen.

B. Listen again and repeat.

C. Pair work.

A. Listen. Circle the picture.

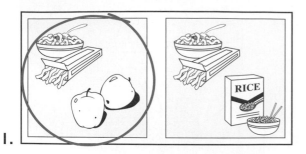

1.

2.

3.

B. Look and listen.

 →  → (image)

C. Listen and respond.

1.

2.

3.

Read and say the words.

  1. bag   rag

  2. leg   peg

  3. dig   pig

  4. jog   log

  5. rug   mug

 6. van   can

  7. bun   gun

  8. dam   jam

  9. gum   sum

 10. sub   tub

  11. lab   cab

  12. sob   job

TEACHER

Literacy: Decode rhyming sounds of one-syllable words with short vowels and final consonants and initial consonants.
More practice: Worksheet 61 (Teacher's Edition CD-ROM).

Read and say the words.

1. map   cap
2. mop   cop
3. fax   wax
4. fix   mix
5. sad   dad
6. bud   mud
7. hat   bat
8. wet   jet
9. cot   pot
10. frog   smog
11. crop   stop
12. clip   slip

Talk about the pictures. Role-play conversations.

TEACHER

Survival / civics review: Point and name things in the pictures. Make sentences about the pictures. Role-play conversations based on the pictures.
Listening-speaking tests: Teacher's Edition CD-ROM.

A. Read and say the words.

1. jog   log   2. hat   bat   3. sit   hit

B. Read and say the words.

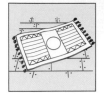   

1. rug   rag   2. fax   fix   3. bud   bed

C. Read and say the words.

1. bun	2. dam	3. pig	4. jam	5. mud
6. cup	7. hut	8. gas	9. crab	10. wet
11. pin	12. bag	13. yes	14. stop	15. drip
16. spot	17. swim	18. plum	19. smog	20. tux

TEACHER

Literacy review: Recognize and decode rhyming and non-rhyming one-syllable words with short vowels, final consonants, and initial consonants and consonant blends.
More practice: Worksheet 63 (Teacher's Edition CD-ROM).
Tests: Teacher's Edition CD-ROM.

🎧 **A. Look and listen.**

1. living room

2. bedroom

3. laundry room

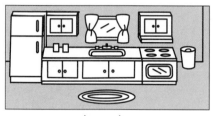

4. kitchen

5. dining room

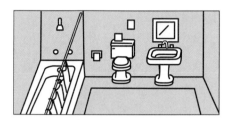

6. bathroom

🎧 **B. Listen again and repeat.**

C. Match the picture and the word.

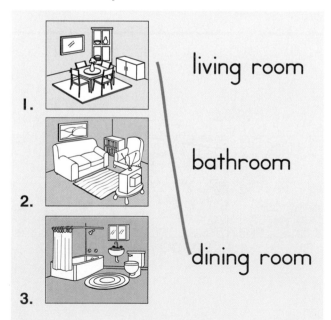

1.

living room

2.

bathroom

3.

dining room

4.

bedroom

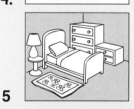

5

kitchen

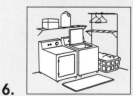

6.

laundry room

TEACHER

Survival: Learn names of rooms in the house.
New language: Living room, bedroom, laundry room, kitchen, dining room, bathroom.

A. Look and listen.

I.

2.

3.

B. Listen again and repeat.

C. Pair work.

MEG   LEN   RON

TEACHER

Survival: Discuss location of another person in another room. Express a belief.
New language: Where's [Ted]? / I think he's [she's] in the [kitchen].

🎧 **A. Look and listen.**

-nd

hand

land

-nk

bank

tank

-nt

dent

rent

-mp

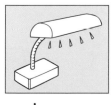
lamp

stamp

🎧 **B. Listen again and repeat.**

C. Read and say the words.

band

sank

tent

camp

TEACHER

Literacy: Decode one-syllable words with short vowels and final consonant blends -nd, -nk, -nt, -mp. Produce corresponding sounds in new words.
More practice: Worksheet 64 (Teacher's Edition CD-ROM).

🎧 **A. Look and listen.**

-lt

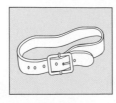

belt

melt

-ft

gift

lift

-st

rest

vest

-sk

ask

mask

🎧 **B. Listen again and repeat.**

C. Read and say the words.

1. melt   2. gift   3. rest   4. mask

TEACHER

Literacy: Decode one-syllable words with short vowels and final consonant blends -lt, -ft, -st, -sk.
More practice: Worksheets 65–66 (Teacher's Edition CD-ROM).

🎧 A. Look and listen.

1. a husband   2. a wife   3. a father   4. a mother   5. a daughter   6. a son

7. single   8. married   9. divorced   10. widowed

🎧 B. Listen again and repeat.

🎧 C. Listen. Circle the picture.

1.

2.

3.

4.

A. Look and listen.

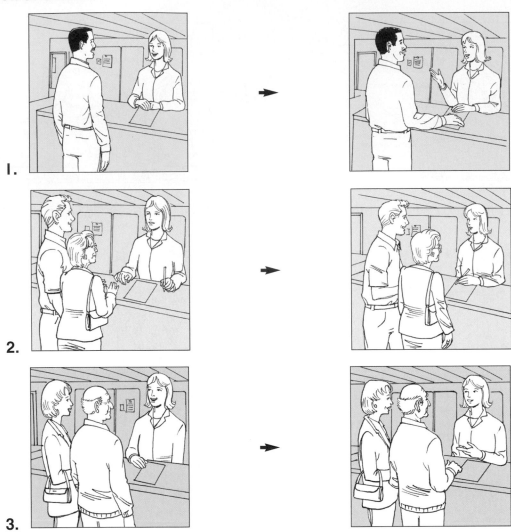

1.

2.

3.

B. Listen again and repeat.

C. Pair work.

Survival: Provide a social security number and marital status.
Civics concepts: Expect to provide social security number and marital status in public offices.
Take responsibility for members of family.
New language: Social security number, marital status, his, her / This is my [mother].

A. Look and listen.

first name   last name

 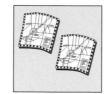   

map   maps   hat   hats

B. Listen again and repeat.

C. Read and say the words.

pot   pots   cop   cops

D. Look and listen.

mug   mugs   pin   pins

E. Listen again and repeat.

F. Read and say the words.

rag   rags   can   cans

TEACHER

Literacy: Decode one-syllable plurals, both voiceless and voiced.
More practice: Worksheet 67 (Teacher's Edition CD-ROM).

🎧 **A. Look and listen.**

-ff

cuff   cliff

-ss

dress   glass

-ll

bell   hill

-ck

rock   clock

🎧 **B. Listen again and repeat.**

C. Read and say the words.

class   smell   truck   block

TEACHER

Literacy: Decode one-syllable words with short vowels and final double consonants
-ff, -ss, -ll, as well as -ck. Produce corresponding sounds in new words.
More practice: Worksheet 68 (Teacher's Edition CD-ROM).

🎧 A. Look and listen.

1. at work　　　　　**2. at school**　　　　　**3. outside**

🎧 B. Listen again and repeat.

🎧 C. Look and listen.

1.  ➡

2. ➡

🎧 D. Listen again and repeat.

E. Pair work.

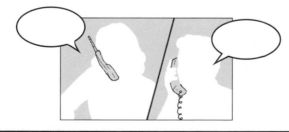

A. Look and listen.

1.

2.

B. Listen again and repeat.

C. Pair work. Use the names.

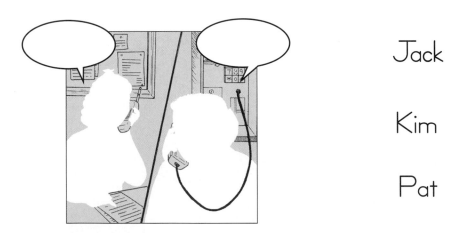

Jack

Kim

Pat

TEACHER

Survival: Answer a phone at work. Express lack of understanding.
Civics concepts: Ask who's calling so you can let the called person know. Inform your employer when you're going to be late.
New language: Who's calling? / I don't understand. / I'm going to be late.

A. Look and listen.

sh–

ship

shop

ch–

chip

chop

qu–

quit

quilt

 B. Listen again and repeat.

C. Read and say the words.

ı. chop   2. ship   3. quit   4. quilt

TEACHER

Literacy: Decode one-syllable words with short vowels and initial digraphs sh-, ch-, qu-.
More practice: Worksheet 69 (Teacher's Edition CD-ROM).

A. Look and listen.

th-

this

B. Listen again and repeat.

C. Read and say the word.

that

D. Look and listen.

th-

think

E. Listen again and repeat.

F. Read and say the word.

thank

Literacy: Decode one-syllable words with short vowels and voiced and voiceless th-.
More practice: Worksheet 70 (Teacher's Edition CD-ROM).

TEACHER

 A. Look and listen.

1.

MESSAGE

To _____
Date _____ Time _____ A.M. ☐ P.M. ☐
M _____
Phone _____
  Area code   Number   Extension

2.

MESSAGE

To _Beth Chan_
Date _____ Time _____ A.M. ☐ P.M. ☐
M _S. Quinn Glass_
Phone _232-1755_
  Area code   Number   Extension

B. Listen again and repeat.

C. Pair work.

TEACHER

Survival: Offer to take a message. Leave a message.
Civics concept: Always offer to take a message for a person who's not there.
New language: Would you like to leave a message?

🎧 A. Listen. Circle the name.

1. ⬭Len Raft⬭ | Len Rask

2. Tom Fist | Tom Fisk

3. Nan Kemp | Nan Kent

4. Jen Lunt | Jen Lund

🎧 B. Look and listen.

➡️

🎧 C. Listen and respond.

1.

2.

3.

🎧 **A. Look and listen.**

-sh

fish

trash

-ch

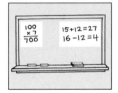

lunch

bench

-th

math

bath

🎧 **B. Listen again and repeat.**

C. Read and say the words.

1. trash

2. lunch

3. bath

TEACHER

Literacy: Decode one-syllable words with short vowels and final digraphs -sh, -ch, -th.
More practice: Worksheet 71 (Teacher's Edition CD-ROM).

A. Look and read.

Beth	Rush	6/27/69
first name	last name	date of birth

M /F   ☑ single ☐ married   000-30-6900
sex   marital status   social security number

Beth Rush
signature

SOCIAL SECURITY

000-30-6900
THIS NUMBER HAS BEEN ESTABLISHED FOR
BETH RUSH

Beth Rush
SIGNATURE

Chuck	Shapp	7/14/55
first name	last name	date of birth

Ⓜ/ F   ☐ single ☑ married   000-76-0513
sex   marital status   social security number

Chuck Shapp
signature

SOCIAL SECURITY

000-76-0513
THIS NUMBER HAS BEEN ESTABLISHED FOR
CHUCK SHAPP

Chuck Shapp
SIGNATURE

B. Fill in the form with your own information.

_____	_____	_____
first name	last name	date of birth

M / F   ☐ single ☐ married   _____
sex   marital status   social security number

_____
signature

TEACHER

Literacy: Read, understand, and fill out a form requesting personal information, including gender.
More practice: Worksheet 72 (Teacher's Edition CD-ROM).

Talk about the pictures. Role-play conversations.

Survival / civics review: Point and name things in the pictures. Make sentences about the pictures. Role-play conversations based on the pictures.
Listening-speaking tests: Teacher's Edition CD-ROM.

TEACHER

UNIT 7 • 133

Read and say the words.

ramp

send

sink

plant

left

list

desk

grass

lock

clocks

quiz

shell

chin

dish

path

ranch

TEACHER

Literacy review: Review decoding of one-syllable words with short vowels and initial and final consonant blends and digraphs.
More practice: Worksheets 73–74 (Teacher's Edition CD-ROM).
Tests: Teacher's Edition CD-ROM.

🎧 A. Look and listen.

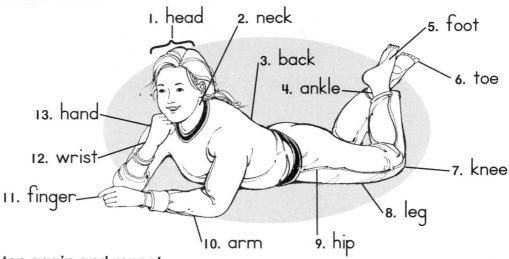

1. head
2. neck
3. back
4. ankle
5. foot
6. toe
7. knee
8. leg
9. hip
10. arm
11. finger
12. wrist
13. hand

🎧 B. Listen again and repeat.

🎧 C. Listen and circle.

1. leg | toe
2. arm | hand
3. ankle | hip
4. neck | leg

🎧 D. Read and listen.

What happened?

I broke my arm.

Oh, no! I'm sorry.

It's OK. Thanks.

🎧 E. Listen again and repeat.

TEACHER

Survival: Learn vocabulary for parts of the body. Describe an injury. Inquire about a misfortune.
Civics concepts: Show interest in others. Accept sympathy.
New language: Head, neck, back, ankle, foot, toe, knee, leg, hip, arm, finger, wrist, hand /
What happened? / I broke my [arm]. / Oh no. I'm sorry. / It's OK. Thanks.

🎧 A. Look and listen.

1. a cold 　2. an upset stomach 　3. a headache 　4. a fever

🎧 B. Listen again and repeat.

🎧 C. Read and listen.

Beck Hardware.

Hello. This is Trish Vox.

Hi Trish. This is Bill.

Hi Bill. I have a fever. I can't come in today.

I'm sorry. Well, feel better soon.

Thanks.

🎧 D. Listen again and repeat.

E. Pair work.

A. Look at the signs.

1. DANGER

2. POISON

3. FLAMMABLE

4. NO SMOKING

5. CAUTION

B. Match.

1.

2.

3.

NO SMOKING

CAUTION

POISON

TEACHER

Literacy: Identify and understand safety and warning symbols.

A. Look at the signs.

1. STOP

2. SLOW

3. SPEED LIMIT

4. SCHOOL ZONE

5. RAILROAD CROSSING

6. HOSPITAL

B. Look at the pictures. Circle the signs.

1.     

2.     

3.

TEACHER

Literacy: Read and interpret common traffic signs.
More practice: Worksheet 75 (Teacher's Edition CD-ROM).

138 • UNIT 8

A. Look and listen.

1. a fire

2. an accident

3. a fire truck

4. an ambulance

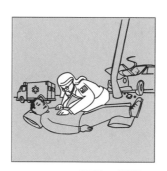

5. an EMT

B. Listen again and repeat.

C. Listen. Circle the picture.

1.

2.

3.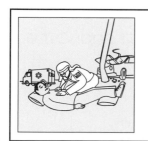

4.

TEACHER

Survival: Learn names of emergency vehicles and medical personnel.
New language: A fire, an accident, a fire truck, an ambulance, an EMT.

A. Read and listen.

I.

2.

B. Listen again and repeat.

C. Listen again. Circle the place.

1. Where's the accident?

| On Glen Street. | On Main Street. |

2. Where's the fire?

| 63 Bank Street. | 78 West Street. |

D. Pair work.

92 Grand Street

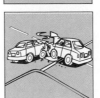

Bliss Street

🎧 A. Read and listen.

1.

2.

3.

4.

5.

B. Circle the words.

1.

Slow down!	Stop!

2.

Slow down!	Stop!

3.

Slow down!	Stop!

TEACHER

Literacy: Read and interpret common traffic safety signs.
More practice: Worksheet 76 (Teacher's Edition CD-ROM).

Look at the pictures. Circle the signs.

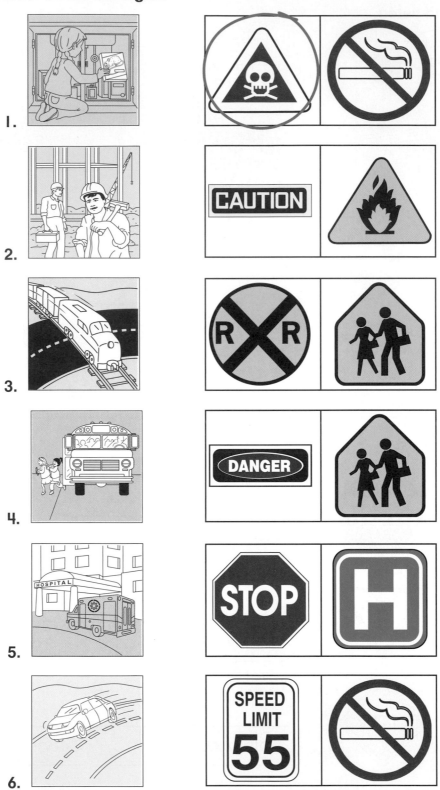

TEACHER

Literacy: Demonstrate understanding of common warning, safety, and road signs.
More practice: Worksheet 77 (Teacher's Edition CD-ROM).

🎧 A. Look and listen.

1. an emergency room

2. a clinic

Bell City Hospital 🚑

Emergency Room

Patient Information:

Name: _____

3. a form

🎧 B. Listen again and repeat.

🎧 C. Read and listen.

Good morning. What's the problem?

I have a cold and a fever.

10:20 AM

OK. Please have a seat and fill out this form.

1.

Good afternoon. What's the problem?

My mother has a fever.

3:36 PM

OK. Please have a seat and fill out this form.

2.

Good evening. What's the problem?

My son has an upset stomach.

8:15 PM

OK. Please have a seat and fill out this form.

3.

🎧 D. Listen again and repeat.

E. Pair work.

8:05 AM

1:25 PM

7:45 PM

TEACHER

Survival: Names of healthcare facilities. State a medical problem.
Civics concept: Provide personal information at the admitting desk of a healthcare facility.
New language: An emergency room, a clinic, a form, has / Please have a seat and fill out this form.

🎧 A. Look and listen.

1. a doctor   **2.** a nurse   **3.** a dentist   **4.** a technician

🎧 B. Listen again and repeat.

🎧 C. Read and listen.

Here's the form.

Thanks. The doctor can see you now.

1.

Here's the form.

Thanks. The dentist can see you now.

2.

Here's the form.

Thanks. The technician can see you now.

3.

🎧 D. Listen again and repeat.

E. Pair work.

A. Copy the capital and lowercase letters.

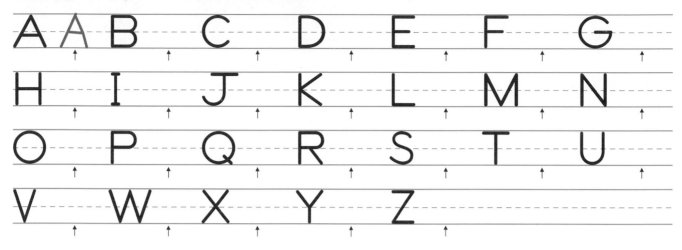

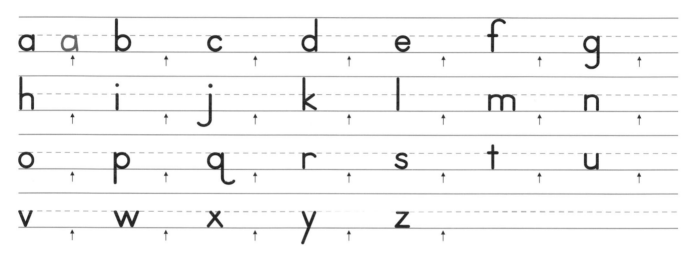

B. Look at the name.

Dennis
first name

Chen
last name

C. Copy the names. Use capital and lowercase letters.

1. jon block Jon Block

2. meg pitt _____

D. Write your name. Use capital and lowercase letters.

first name   last name

TEACHER

Literacy: Review the capital and lowercase letters. Write your name in capital and lowercase letters.
More practice: Worksheet 78 (Teacher's Edition CD-ROM).

A. Circle or cross out.

1. _____   ✗ _____   ___ⓐ_____

✗ Jeff

2. _____   Jeff _____   _____

Jeff

3. _Kim Banks_   Kim _____Banks_   _Kim_____

Banks

4. _____   Ted Kroff _____   _Ted Kroff_

Ted Kroff

B. Write your name on the line.

_____

name

C. Write your first name and last name on the line.

_____

first name   last name

TEACHER

Literacy: Write on the line, not above or below the line.
More practice: Worksheet 79 (Teacher's Edition CD-ROM).

146 • UNIT 8

A. Look and listen.

1. a seat belt

2. a car seat

3. a safety harness

B. Listen again and repeat.

C. Read and listen.

You have to use a seat belt.

Why?

Because it's the law.

1.

You have to use a car seat.

Why?

Because it's the law.

2.

D. Listen again and repeat.

E. Pair work.

TEACHER

Survival: State a necessity. Ask for and provide a reason.

Civics concept: There are laws requiring seat belt use and safety restraints. Observe the law.

New language: A seat belt, a car seat, a safety harness / You have to [use a seat belt]. / Why? / Because it's the law.

A. Listen. Circle the picture.

1.

2.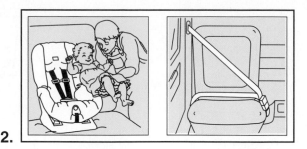

3.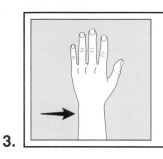

B. Look and listen.

C. Listen and respond.

1.

2.

3.

A. Look at the name.

| W | I | L | L | ▉ | C | O | X | | | | |

Full name

B. Write your full name. Leave a space.

| | | | | | | | | | | | |

Full name

C. Fill out the forms. Use capital letters and lowercase letters. Leave a space.

Bell Hospital
Emergency Room

Full Name:

ⓛ Longview Health Center   Emergency Room

_____   _____
first name   last name

🦷 Dental Clinic   Emergency Visit

_____   _____
last name   first name

TEACHER

Literacy: Understand that full name means first and last names. Separate first and last name with a space.
More practice: Worksheet 80 (Teacher's Edition CD-ROM).

Copy the words on the line. Leave a space between words.

 1. acold

  a cold

 2. afever

 3. anarm

 4. SCHOOLZONE

 5. adoctor

 6. anurse

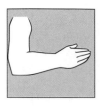 7. afire

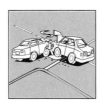 8. anaccident

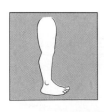 9. aleg

 10. NOSMOKING

Talk about the picture. Role-play conversations.

A. Copy the words on the lines. Leave a space between words.

1. railroadcrossing   _railroad crossing_

2. schoolzone

3. adentist

4. anEMT

5. anambulance

B. Copy the names on the lines. Leave a space between first and last names.

1. MegPitt   _Meg Pitt_

2. LinBanks

3. RobWest

4. PamGrant

C. Copy the names on the lines. Use capital and lowercase letters.

1. sherri smith   _Sherri Smith_

2. matt dash

3. dennis chen

4. jill nott

UNIT 9

🎧 A. Look at the bills. Listen.

1. $1.00

2. $5.00

3. $10.00

4. $20.00

5. $50.00

6. $100.00

🎧 B. Listen again and repeat.

🎧 C. Read and listen.

Excuse me. Do you have change for $20?

Just a minute. I'll check.

Yes, I do. Here you go.

Thanks.

🎧 D. Listen again and repeat.

E. Pair work. Ask for change.

⌒ A. Look at the coins. Listen.

1. $.01

2. $.05

3. $.10

4. $.25

5. $.50

6. $1.00

⌒ B. Listen again and repeat.

⌒ C. Read and listen.

Excuse me. Do you have change for a dollar?

Sure. Are dimes OK?

Actually, I need quarters for the meter.

Sorry.

⌒ D. Listen again and repeat.

A. Read and listen.

1. $2.20   2. $6.78   3. $41.05   4. $12.90

B. Listen again and repeat.

C. Pair work. Say each amount both ways.

Three dollars and thirty-two cents.

Three thirty-two.

$3.32

$7.50 $45.99

$10.15 $98.45

TEACHER

Literacy: Learn how to read and say dollar and cents amounts in two ways. ["Five dollars and fifty cents" and "Five-fifty," for example.]

🎧 **A. Listen. Circle the amount.**

1. ($14.44) | $14.14   2. $32.45 | $23.45   3. $76.09 | $67.90

4. $9.99 | $9.09   5. $2.16 | $2.60   6. $7.23 | $.23

B. Look. Write the amount.

1. $ 2.50

2. $ .02

3. $15.

4. $2.0

5. $ 0.

6. $ 5.

🎧 **C. Listen to the conversations. Write the amount.**

1. $ 6.00   2. $.   3. $.

TEACHER

Literacy: Understand spoken monetary amounts. Write dollar and cent amounts heard. Understand and use the decimal point between the dollars and cents.
More practice: Worksheet 83 (Teacher's Edition CD-ROM).

🎧 A. Read and listen.

🎧 B. Listen again and repeat.

C. Pair work. Ask about the rent.

A. Look and listen.

1. a lease   2. a water bill   3. a cable bill

4. a telephone bill   5. a gas and electric bill

B. Listen again and repeat.

C. Read and listen.

How much is the rent?

$500 a month. That includes gas and electric.

And what about cable?

Let's check the lease.

D. Listen again and repeat.

E. Pair work. Ask about utilities.

Public Gas and Electric Company

Cable TV Company

Telephone Company

Circle the picture.

1. $40.00
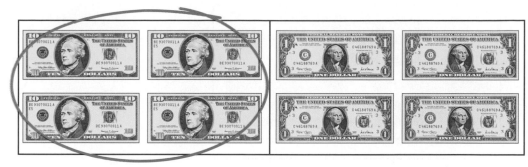

2. $16.00

3. $.33
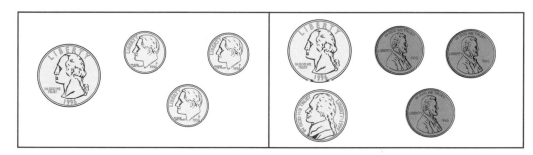

4. $6.11

5. $21.26
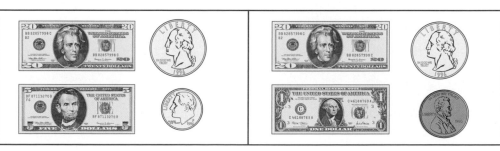

TEACHER

Literacy: Choose ways to make up whole dollar amounts, whole cents amounts, and dollar and cents amounts.
More practice: Worksheet 84 (Teacher's Edition CD-ROM).

Circle the amount.

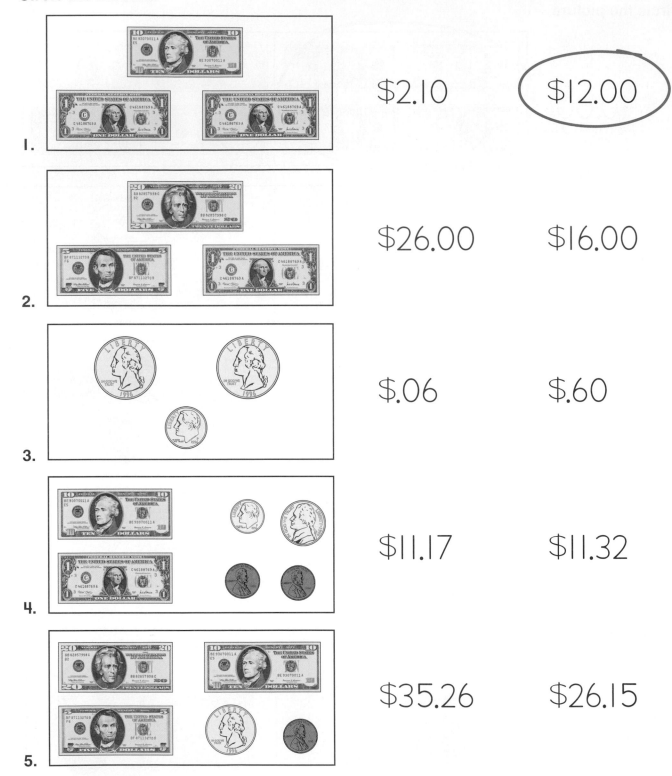

1. $2.10   ($12.00)

2. $26.00 $16.00

3. $.06 $.60

4. $11.17 $11.32

5. $35.26 $26.15

TEACHER

Literacy: Understand decimal representation of combinations of coins and bills.
More practice: Worksheet 85 (Teacher's Edition CD-ROM).

🎧 A. Look and listen.

1. pay	2. cash	3. I.D.	4. a receipt

 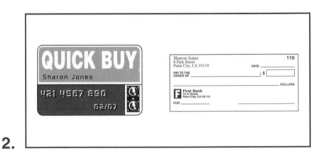

5. a credit card	6. a check	7. a money order

🎧 B. Listen again and repeat.

🎧 C. Listen. Circle the picture.

 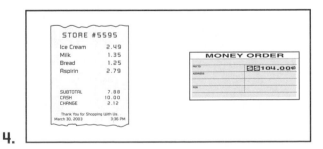

1.

2.

3.

4.

TEACHER

Survival: Identify means of payment.
Civics concept: There are a variety of ways to pay.
New Language: Pay, cash, I.D., a receipt, a credit card, a check, a money order.

A. Read and listen.

B. Listen again and repeat.

C. Pair work. Talk about paying bills.

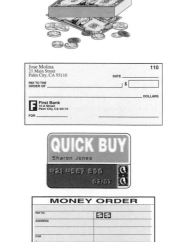

Match the bill and the payment.

1.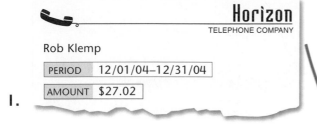

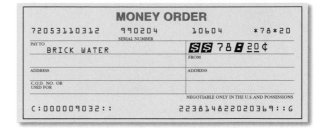

2.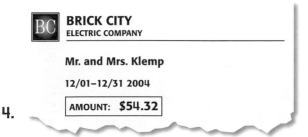

3.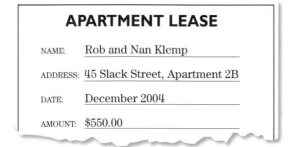

4. BRICK CITY

ELECTRIC COMPANY

Mr. and Mrs. Klemp

12/01–12/31 2004

AMOUNT: **$54.32**

TEACHER

Literacy: Recognize checks, money orders, and cash payments for rent and utility bills.
More Practice: Worksheet 86 (Teacher's Edition CD-ROM).

A. Look at the cable bill. Look at the envelope.

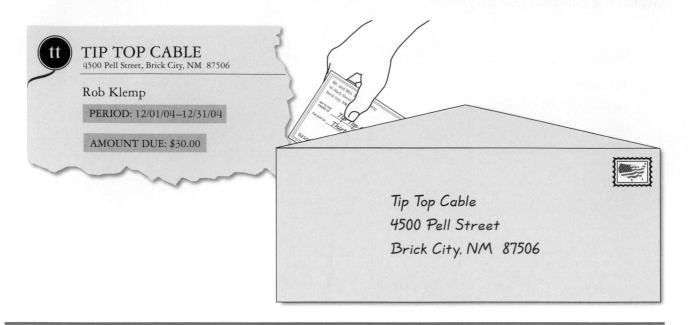

TIP TOP CABLE
4500 Pell Street, Brick City, NM 87506

Rob Klemp

PERIOD: 12/01/04–12/31/04

AMOUNT DUE: $30.00

Tip Top Cable
4500 Pell Street
Brick City, NM 87506

B. Read the bill. Trace the name and address on the envelope.

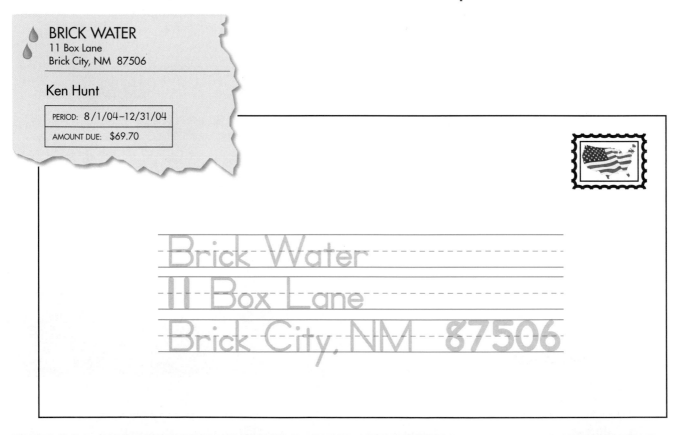

BRICK WATER
11 Box Lane
Brick City, NM 87506

Ken Hunt

PERIOD: 8/1/04–12/31/04

AMOUNT DUE: $69.70

Brick Water
11 Box Lane
Brick City, NM 87506

Literacy: Address an envelope.
More Practice: Worksheet 87 (Teacher's Edition CD-ROM).

TEACHER

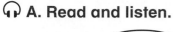
A. Read and listen.

1.

2.

B. Listen again and repeat.

C. Pair work. Pay. Get a receipt. Show I.D.

Sharon Jones
8 Park Street
Palm City, CA 93110   **110**

DATE _____

PAY TO THE
ORDER OF _____ | $ [   ]

_____ DOLLARS

First Bank
10 A Street
Palm City, CA 93110

FOR _____   _____

QUICK BUY
Jose Molina
123 4567 890
02/07

```
*************************************
                           $5.50
                        + $2.23
          TOTAL           $7.73
*************************************
```

 **A. Listen. Circle the words.**

1.
| (cash) | check |

2.
| cash | check |

3.
| cash | I.D. |

4.
| check | credit card |

5.
| cash | receipt |

🎧 **B. Look and listen.**

🎧 **C. Listen and respond.**

1.   2.   3.

TEACHER

Authentic practice: Students listen to an authentic conversation about payment and then complete listening and speaking tasks, providing their own information.

A. Read the name and address on the envelope.

Ann Pinks
90 Pack Street
Glendale, CA 91223

B. Look at the form. Write the name and address on the envelope.

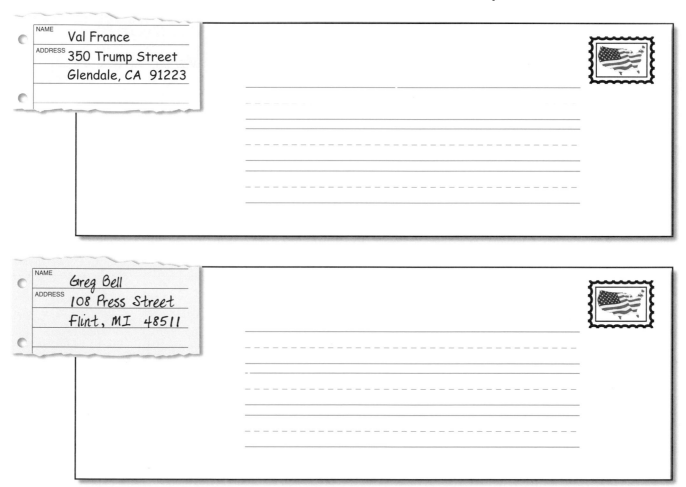

NAME Val France
ADDRESS 350 Trump Street
Glendale, CA 91223

NAME Greg Bell
ADDRESS 108 Press Street
Flint, MI 48511

TEACHER

Literacy: Address an envelope properly with capital and lowercase letters, spaces, and in three lines.
More practice: Worksheet 88 (Teacher's Edition CD-ROM).

A. Copy the sentences. Put spaces between the words.

1. Ipaybymail.   I pay by mail.

2. Hereyougo.   _____

3. Shehasafever.   _____

B. Copy the sentences. Use a capital letter.

1. he has a cold.   He has a cold.

2. she needs a dime.   _____

3. i like this house.   _____

4. i pay by check.   _____

5. my son has a car.   _____

6. my name is Bill.   _____

TEACHER

Literacy: Sentences are made of words. Spaces separate the words from each other. Sentences begin with a capital letter.
More practice: Worksheet 89 (Teacher's Edition CD-ROM).

Talk about the pictures. Role-play conversations.

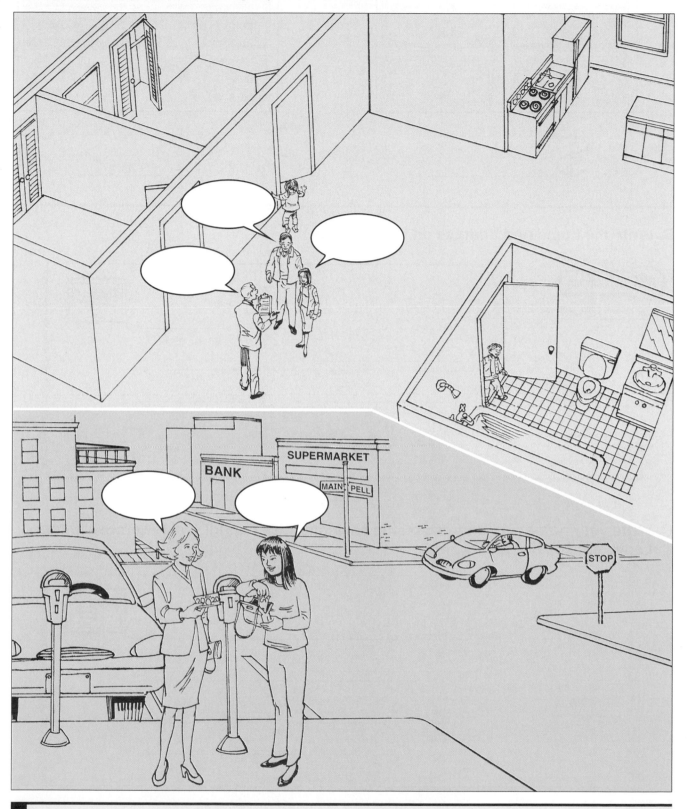

A. Write the amount.

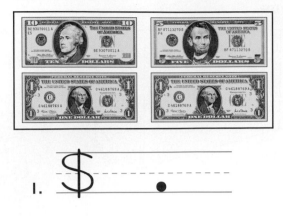

1. $ \$ \underline{\hspace{2cm}} \bullet $

2. $ \$ \underline{\hspace{2cm}} \bullet $

B. Write the name and address on the envelope.

ABC Gas Company
2 Mack Drive, Grant, NJ 07078

C. Write <u>your</u> name and address on the envelope. Use capital and lowercase letters. Leave spaces between words.

🎧 **A. Look and listen.**

occupations

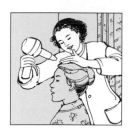

1. a hairdresser

2. a manicurist

3. a barber

4. a cook

5. a babysitter

6. a porter   7. a parking attendant   8. a delivery driver

🎧 **B. Listen again and repeat.**

C. Look at the picture. Read. Circle the letter.

1. She's a _____.
   (a.) babysitter
   b. manicurist

2. He's a _____.
   a. barber
   b. porter

3. She's a _____.
   a. cook
   b. hairdresser

TEACHER

Survival: Learn names of occupations.
New language: A hairdresser, a manicurist, a barber, a cook, a babysitter, a porter, a parking attendant, a delivery driver.

A. Look and listen.

workplaces

1. a beauty salon

2. a barber shop

3. a restaurant

4. a private home

5. a hotel

6. a day care center

7. a warehouse

8. an office building

B. Listen again and repeat.

C. Read and listen.

Yes, I am.

Are you employed?

1.

Where do you work?

In a restaurant.

Are you employed?

No, I'm not. I'm unemployed right now.

2.

D. Listen again and repeat.

E. Pair work. Talk about work.

 **A. Look and listen.**

 ar

car   park   arm

B. Listen again and repeat.

C. Read and say the words.

card   barn   cart

D. Look and listen.

or

fork   corn

E. Listen again and repeat.

F. Read and say the words.

horn   torn   fort

🎧 **A. Look and listen.**

ir   skirt   bird

ur   turn   hurt

er   fern   herd

🎧 **B. Listen again and repeat.**

C. Read and say the words.

shirt   stir   girl   burn   curl

A. Look and listen.

job skills

"My name is Elena Silva."

1. speak English

HELP WANTED
SUPERMARKET
CALL
982-4513

2. read

Boris Chanko
Name

Address

3. write

B. Listen again and repeat.

C. Read and listen.

"Can you speak English?" "Yes, I can." "And can you read and write?" "Yes, a little." "What other languages can you speak?" "I can speak Spanish."

D. Listen again and repeat.

E. Pair work. Talk about job skills.

⌒ A. Look and listen.

more job skills

1. drive

2. cut hair

3. cook

4. clean

5. take care of children

⌒ B. Listen again and repeat.

⌒ C. Read and listen.

What skills do you have?

I can drive.

And what other skills do you have?

I can cook and I can take care of children.

⌒ D. Listen again and repeat.

E. Pair work. Talk about more job skills.

TEACHER

Survival: Describe one's job skills.

Civics concept: Matching your skills to those required on a job is important to finding employment.

New language: Cut hair, cook, clean, take care of children / What [other] skills do you have? / I can [cook].

176 • UNIT 10

🎧 **A. Look and listen.**

a

plane   tape

🎧 **B. Listen again and repeat.**

C. Read and say the words.

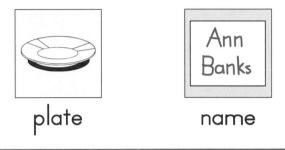

plate   name

🎧 **D. Look and listen.**

i

nine   five

🎧 **E. Listen again and repeat.**

F. Read and say the words.

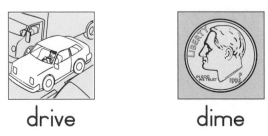

drive   dime

TEACHER

Literacy: Understand that letters represent more than one sound. Decode one-syllable words with long vowel–consonant–silent -e combination.
More practice: Worksheet 93 (Teacher's Edition CD-ROM).

🎧 **A. Look and listen.**

o   robe   home

u   June   flute

🎧 **B. Listen again and repeat.**

C. Read and say the words.

stove   bone   rule   prune

D. Read and say the words.

1. tap tape   2. pin pine   3. rob robe   4. tub tube

TEACHER

Literacy: Decode one-syllable words with long vowel–consonant–silent -e combination. Distinguish between words with short vowels and words with long vowel–consonant–silent -e combination.
More practice: Worksheet 94 (Teacher's Edition CD-ROM).

🎧 **A. Read and listen.**

🎧 **B. Listen again and repeat.**

C. Pair work. Talk about changing jobs.

TEACHER

Survival: State desire to change jobs. Express job preferences.

Civics concepts: You can change to a better job. There are opportunities for advancement at many workplaces.

New language: I'd like to change jobs. / Right now I'm a [parking attendant]. / I'd like to be a [cook].

A. Look and listen.

NAME	Alma Brown
PHONE	(201) 555-6733
NAME	Jack Jensen
PHONE	(201) 555-5544

Employment Application

ACE COMPANY

Date: _____

NAME: _____   OCCUPATION: _____
    Last Name   First Name

ADDRESS: _____
    Number and Street   City   State   ZIP Code

1. references

2. an application

B. Listen again and repeat.

C. Read and listen.

1. Do you have any experience in this country? — Yes, I do.

Do you have any references? — Yes. Here's the list.

That's great. Here's an application.

What skills do you have?

2. Do you have any experience in this country? — No, I don't.

That's great. Here's an application. — I can drive.

D. Listen again and repeat.

E. Pair work. Talk about experience and references.

My name is Elena Silva.

🎧 **A. Look and listen.**

ou

cloud

house

🎧 **B. Listen again and repeat.**

C. Read and say the words.

count

mouth

🎧 **D. Look and listen.**

ow

down

cow

🎧 **E. Listen again and repeat.**

F. Read and say the words.

town

owl

TEACHER

Literacy: Decode one-syllable words with homophonic diphthongs ou and ow.
More practice: Worksheet 95 (Teacher's Edition CD-ROM).

A. Look and listen.

oi

coin

boil

oy

boy

toy

B. Listen again and repeat.

C. Read and say the words.

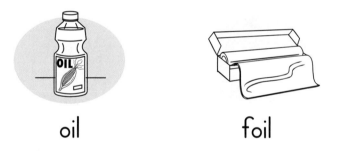

oil

foil

D. Read and say the words.

1. count   house
2. oil   foil
3. down   town
4. toy   boy
5. cloud   mouth

A. Read and listen.

B. Listen again and repeat.

C. Read and listen.

D. Listen again and repeat.

E. Pair work. Talk about your job history.

🎧 **A. Listen. Circle the letter.**

1. (a.) She works in a restaurant.   b. She works in a hotel.

2. a. He wants to be a cook.   b. He wants to be a barber.

3. a. She can drive.   b. She can cook.

🎧 **B. Look and listen.**

🎧 **C. Listen and respond.**

1.

2.

3.

TEACHER

Authentic practice: Students listen to an authentic conversation about experience and job skills and then complete listening and speaking tasks, providing true information.

184 • UNIT 10

A. Look at the sentence.

capital letter   period

She is a cook.

B. Copy the sentences. Use capital letters. Use periods.

1. i can read <u>   I can read.   </u>

2. he can write <u>   </u>

3. he is a porter <u>   </u>

4. she is a manicurist <u>   </u>

5. i can speak English <u>   </u>

6. my son has a cold <u>   </u>

C. Copy the sentences. Leave a space after the period.

1. I can speak English.I can speak Spanish.

   <u>   I can speak English. I can speak Spanish.   </u>

2. My mother is a doctor.She is at home right now.

   <u>   </u>

3. Mark is a delivery driver.He works in a warehouse.

   <u>   </u>

TEACHER

Literacy: Sentences are made of words. Sentences begin with a capital letter and end with a period. There's a space between sentences.
More practice: Worksheet 97 (Teacher's Edition CD-ROM).

A. Read the job application.

City of Round Point
Application for employment

Loy   Tan
first name   middle name   last name

3/12/68   marital status ☐ single ☑ married   sex ☑ male   ☐ female
date of birth

127 Harvard Lane   Mount Soyer, Alabama   36701
address   number and street   city and state   zip code

(251) 555-4231   000369821
area code and phone number   social security number

Are you employed?   ☑ yes   ☐ no   Where: Ben's Warehouse

Skills: Check those that apply   read English ☑   write English ☑   speak English ☑   drive ☐

Do you have references? ☑ yes   ☐ no

Loy Tan   11/14/04
signature   date

B. Do it yourself. Fill out the application.

City of Round Point
Application for employment

_____   _____   _____
first name   middle name   last name

_____   marital status ☐ single   ☐ married   sex ☐ male   ☐ female
date of birth

_____   _____   _____
address   number and street   city and state   zip code

_____   _____
area code and phone number   social security number

Are you employed?   ☐ yes   ☐ no   Where: _____

Skills: Check those that apply   read English ☐   write English ☐   speak English ☐   drive ☐

Do you have references? ☐ yes   ☐ no

_____   _____
signature   date

Talk about the pictures. Role-play conversations.

A. Read and say the words.

1. barn   2. fort   3. stir   4. burn   5. fern

6. nameplate   7. fine   8. home   9. June   10. house

11. down   12. downtown   13. coin   14. boy

B. Copy the sentences. Use a capital letter. Use a period. Leave a space after the period.

1. he wants a job _____

2. she is a driver _____

3. I speak English.I speak Spanish. _____

_____

C. Fill out the application.

```
_____
first name                    middle name                        last name

_____ / _____ / _____        sex    M ☐        F ☐
date of birth

_____
number and street             city and state                     zip code

_____            _____
area code and phone number                           social security number

Are you employed?      yes ☐      no ☐

Skills: Check those that apply        read English ☐      write English ☐      speak English ☐      drive ☐

Do you have references?      yes ☐      no ☐

_____    _____ / _____ / _____
signature                                            date
```

Literacy review: Decode words with r-controlled vowels, long vowels followed by consonants and mute e, and diphthongs. Begin sentences with a capital letter and end with a period. Leave a space between sentences. Fill out a job application with personal information.
More practice: Worksheets 99–100 (Teacher's Edition CD-ROM).
Tests: Teacher's Edition CD-ROM.

TEACHER

Sequential index of phonics principles

The words included in this list are taken from the units in which each phonics principle is presented. All words are illustrated on the Student's Book pages.

Initial Consonants (unit 4)

s–	small	b–	button	d–	discount store	r–	raincoat
m–	medium	p–	pants	g–	garage	w–	watch
l–	large	v–	vest	h–	hardware store	y–	yarn
t–	tie	k–	key	n–	newsstand	f–	fabric
c–	collar	z–	zipper	j–	jacket		

Short vowels (unit 5)

a		e		i		o		u	
	hat		ten		pit		hot		sun
	rat		pen		mitt		pot		bun
	cat		men		kit		cot		run
	bat		hen		sit		dot		gun
	mat				hit		tot		fun

Initial Consonant blends (unit 5)

cr–	crab	tr–	track	gl–	glass	sk–	skin
	crib		truck	sl–	sled	sm–	smog
	crop		trap	cl–	clip	sp–	spot
dr–	dress	fr–	frog	bl–	block	st–	stop
	drip		fridge	pl–	plum	sw–	swim
	drum	br–	branch				
			bridge				
			brick				

Final consonants (unit 6)

-g		-n		-b		-x		-d	
-g	bag	-n	can	-b	lab	-x	fax	-d	dad
	rag		men		web		fix		bed
	leg		pin		job		box		lid
	peg		bun		sub		tux		nod
	dig		van		cab		wax		mud
	pig		gun		sob		mix		sad
	jog				tub				rod
	log	-m	dam			-t	hat		bud
	rug		rim	-s	gas		wet		
	mug		mom		yes		sit		
	fog		sum				dot		
	big		jam	-p	map		cut		
	hug		gum		lip		bat		
	wag				mop		jet		
					cup		hit		
					cap		pot		
					cop		hut		

Final consonant blends (unit 7)

-nd hand land band send	-mp lamp stamp camp ramp	-sk ask mask desk	-ll bell hill smell shell
-nk bank tank sank sink	-lt belt melt -ft gift lift left	-ff cuff cliff -ss dress glass class grass	-ck rock clock truck block lock
-nt dent rent tent plant	-st rest vest list		

One-syllable plurals (unit 7)

map	maps	pot	pots	mug	mugs	rag	rags
hat	hats	cop	cops	pin	pins	can	cans

Initial digraphs (unit 7)

sh- ship shop shell	ch- chip chop chin	qu- quit quilt quiz	th- this that think thank

Final digraphs (unit 7)

-sh		-ch		-th	
fish		lunch		math	
trash		bench		bath	
dish		ranch		path	

R-controlled vowels (unit 10)

ar		or		ir		ur	
car		fork		skirt		turn	
park		corn		bird		hurt	
arm		horn		shirt		burn	
card		torn		stir		curl	
barn		fort		girl			
cart						er	fern
							herd

Long vowel–consonant–silent -e combinations (unit 10)

a		i		o		u	
plane		nine		robe		June	
tape		five		home		flute	
plate		drive		stove		rule	
name		dime		bone		prune	

Diphthongs (unit 10)

ou		ow		oi		oy	
cloud		down		coin		boy	
house		cow		boil		toy	
count		town		oil			
mouth		owl		foil			

Sequential index of survival language

This is a unit-by-unit list of all the social language from the survival language pages in *Literacy Plus B*.

Welcome

- I'm [Len].
- Nice to meet you [too].

- Bye.
- See you later.

Unit 1

- Hi. I'm [Ted].
- What's your name?
- Thank you.
- You're welcome.
- That's a nice name.
- Thanks!
- What's your first [middle, last] name?
- What do you do?
- I'm a [student].

- What about you?
- And you?
- A [student]?
- Really?
- Yes.
- How are you?
- Fine, thanks.
- Great.

Unit 2

- Excuse me.
- Where's the [post office]?
- It's [right] over there.
- The [library] is next to the [bank].
- It's on [Main Street].
- What's the address?

- What's your zip code?
- I'm looking for [M Street].
- Could you repeat that, please?
- Sure.
- This is [number 10].

Unit 3

- How do I get to the [supermarket]?
- Take the [bus].
- It's [not] far.
- Which [bus] goes to the [hospital]?
- The [3].
- Turn right [left] at the corner.
- Go straight.
- What's your telephone number?
- My number's [555-3211].

- Call [me], please.
- And what's your area code?
- My area code's [935].
- What's the number?
- I don't know.
- I need directions.
- Are you taking the [bus]?
- Take the [5] to [Main Street].

Unit 4

- Can I help you?
- I'm looking for [the ties].
- [The shoes] are across from [the purses].
- Do you have this [these] in [medium] / [size 9]?
- Just a minute. I'll check.

- I'm sorry. We don't.
- Here you go.
- Are you a [salesperson]?
- No problem.
- How is it?
- It's too small / [too large] / [fine].
- I'll take it.

Unit 5

- What time is it?
- It's [9:00].
- Let's [eat].
- When do you [go to school]?
- From [Monday] to [Friday].
- On [Wednesday].
- What are your work hours on [Monday]?
- On [Monday], I work from [9] to [5].

- What time do you [go to work]?
- On [Monday], I go at [9:00].
- It's hot [warm, cold, cool].
- Where are you from?
- I'm from [China].
- What's the weather like in [January]?
- Good morning [afternoon, evening, night].

Unit 6

- What time is [lunch] today?
- At [8:00] [noon].
- [Dinner's] from [6:00] to [7:00].
- What do you eat for [breakfast]?
- I eat [cereal].
- Please pass the [salt].
- Here you are.

- Let's go shopping.
- What do we need?
- Anything else?
- I love [fruit].
- Me too.
- [Vegetables] are good / not good for you.

Unit 7

- Where's [Kim]?
- I think he's / she's in the [living room].
- What's your marital status?
- This is my [mother].
- What's his [her] social security number?
- Hello?
- This is [Tim]. Is [Ann] there?

- He's / she's not here right now.
- I'll call back later / in [10] minutes.
- Who's calling?
- I don't understand.
- I'm going to be late.
- Would you like to leave a message?

Unit 8

- What happened?
- I broke my [arm].
- Oh, no. I'm sorry.
- It's OK. Thanks!
- I have a cold / an upset stomach / a headache / a fever.
- I can't come in today.
- Well, feel better soon.
- 911. What's the problem?
- There's [a fire].
- We need [an ambulance].

- Help!
- Let's get out and call 911.
- Quick!
- Please have a seat and fill out this form.
- Here's the form.
- The [doctor] can see you now.
- You have to [use a seat belt].
- Why?
- Because it's the law.

Unit 9

- Do you have change for [$20]?
- Yes, I do.
- Are [dimes] OK?
- Actually, I need [quarters] for the meter.
- This [apartment] is nice.
- How much is the rent?
- [$450] a month.
- I'll take it.
- I'm sorry. That's too much.

- That includes [gas and electric].
- And what about [cable]?
- Let's check the lease.
- How do you pay your [bills]?
- I pay by check / in cash / with a money order.
- Do you pay by mail?
- May I have a receipt?
- Do you take checks?
- Do you have I.D.?

Unit 10

- Where do you work?
- In a [restaurant].
- Are you employed?
- I'm unemployed right now.
- Can you [speak English]?
- Yes, I can. / Yes, a little.
- What other languages can you speak?
- I can speak [Spanish].
- What [other] skills do you have?
- I can [cook].
- I'd like to change jobs.

- Right now I'm a [parking attendant].
- I'd like to be a [cook].
- Do you have any experience in this country?
- Do you have references?
- Yes. Here's the list.
- What did you do in your country?
- I was [a nurse].
- For how long?
- Excuse me? Could you explain that again?

Alphabetical vocabulary list

This is an alphabetical list of all active vocabulary in *Literacy Plus B*. The numbers refer to the page on which the word first appears. Words appearing in capital letters are sight words.

A

a little 175
accident 139
across the street 32
address 35
afternoon 93
airport 49
AM 99
ambulance 139
ankle 135
apartment 31
apple 107
application 180
April 90
area code 53
arm 135
around the corner 32
at school 125
at work 125
August 90

B

babysitter 171
back 135
banana 107
bank 27
barber 171
barber shop 172
bathroom 117
bean 107
beauty salon 172
bedroom 117
boat 45
bread 103
breakfast 99
bridge 49
bus 45
bus stop 27
butcher 17
butter 104

C

cable bill 158
candy 111
car 45
car seat 147
carrot 107
cash 161
cashier 72
CAUTION 137
cereal 103
check 161
cheese 103
chicken 103
clean 176
clinic 143
coat 63
coffee 104
cold *adj.* 90
cold *n.* 136
cook *n.* 171
cook *v.* 176
cookies 111
cool 90
credit card 161
customer 72
cut hair 176

D

DANGER 137
daughter 121
day 85
day care center 172
December 90
deli 71
delivery driver 171
dentist 144
dime 154
dining room 117
dinner 99
divorced 121
doctor 144
dollar 153
down the street 32
dress 63
drive 46
drugstore 71

E

eat 82
emergency room 143
EMT 139
English 175
evening 93
extra large 67